A
Somerset
Christmas

A
Somerset
Christmas

Compiled by John Chandler

ALAN SUTTON PUBLISHING LIMITED

First published in the United Kingdom in 1994
Alan Sutton Publishing Limited · Phoenix Mill · Far Thrupp
Stroud · Gloucestershire

First published in the United States of America in 1994
Alan Sutton Publishing Inc · 83 Washington Street · Dover
NH 03820

British Library Cataloguing in Publication Data

A catalogue record for this book is available from the
British Library.

ISBN 0-7509-0604-9

Library of Congress Cataloging in Publication Data
applied for

Cover illustration: Kingston, Somerset, *by Charles Leaver
(Sutcliffe Galleries, Harrogate; photograph: Fine Art Photographic
Library Ltd)*

Typeset in Garamond 12/13.
Typesetting and origination by
Alan Sutton Publishing Limited.
Printed in Great Britain by
WBC, Bridgend, Mid Glam.

Contents

Exmoor's Winter Pageant

E.W. HENDY

*Since weather is usually the opening topic of conversation,
between friends or strangers, let us begin our celebration of
Christmas in Somerset with a drift of Exmoor snow. Our
reporter is the naturalist and countryman E.W. Hendy, who
in 1930 brought together a number of his contributions to
newspapers and magazines into a book,* Wild Exmoor
through the Year. *In it he depicts the activities of birds
and animals month by month, with a gift for vivid
description which transports the reader to his side to
experience – in this instance – a December sunrise and
snowfall.*

Winter, amid the moors and coombes of the West, is a time of
happy surprises; for thanks to the mutabilities of our
inconstant climate, it is the unexpected which always happens.
In some years the mellowness of autumn lingers on till within
a week or two of a green Christmas; you may find herb-robert,
mallow, valerian, periwinkle, forget-me-not, campion and
scabious – even a late foxglove – and a dozen other common
flowers in bloom in the hedgerows. A sprig or two of bell-
heather is always to be seen in some sheltered corner. Gorse is
ever in flower, but it was a surprise to see a lady-bird amid its
spikelets in November. I have found my first primrose on
Christmas day.

1

Exmoor after snow

To mankind, winter sunrises are more familiar than those of summer. We wake to find the room flooded with a subdued rosy radiance; above the rim of skyline streaks of tawny orange and glowering red sprawl like the glistening length of some gaudy dragon-salamander. Pines top the ridge in silhouette; below them the still darkened moorland shades from purple into velvety black; the arc above is packed with ruffled clouds, tinged with infinite delicacies of rose, from the faint blush of apple-blossom to the carmine of flamingo's wing; between them are rifts of metallic blue, unfathomably deep. And across this riotous pageant of colour rooks and jackdaws, tossed and buffeted by the wind, steer their clamorous journey to feeding grounds on emerald meadows by the sea's verge.

The country folk describe such a memorable dawn more succinctly; they say 'The reds are out,' and prophesy rain before evening. Often they are right, but it may portend only wind. In any event a change in the weather follows, soon or

late. The next morning you may look out upon a dazzling wonderland of snow. The moor, all its rugged contours smoothed and softened, seems to have drawn nearer during the night, so clear and vivid are its outlines. With glasses, or even with the naked eye, you may see a line of black specks crawling downwards towards the woods which fringe the coombes; they are the red deer seeking the succulent ivy which clothes the stunted oaks; walk through any sheltered woodland and you will find the ivy leaves bitten off as high as a stag can reach, upright on its hind legs: if the snow lasts, deer become so tamed with hunger that they scarcely move at your approach.

On the meadows near the sea, where the snow lies but sparsely, and vanishes most quickly, birds, driven from more northern latitudes by stress of weather, congregate in multitudes – finches, waders, gulls, plover, and thrushes of all species. But the ravens and the rest of the crow tribe still haunt the moorland wastes: deep snow means dead sheep, and where these are the carrion eaters are gathered together.

Walking one morning after a blizzard, I took a pathway which led me down into the Horner Woods, and in a moment I was in a fairy land. Each crinkled branch of stunted oak was limned in snow, and where a cluster of dead leaves had given the flakes a resting place the laden branches were bent and curved; from the ancient oaks and alders which clothe the lower slopes the unwonted burden had ruthlessly torn great limbs. Halting some thirty yards down the path I looked back along an alley completely arched over with crystalline tracery, and at the end of the vista was a glimpse of a glistening waste of moor, rising gently to a sky of a very pale and filmy blue.

Tales of cars and lorries embedded in snowdrifts on the moorland roads led me the next day to climb Porlock Hill and see for myself. As I trudged upwards I began to think that perhaps the stories were exaggerated; the half-thawed surface

Difficult driving conditions during an Exmoor winter

was slippery, but until I reached the one thousand feet line the snow was only an inch or two deep. A two-seater car, containing two cheerful optimists, passed me about half-way up. But, once on Porlock Common, there was a change. Soon I heard the two-seater grunting and groaning; as I came round a corner I saw it endeavouring to back out of a drift. Eventually its efforts were successful, and it retreated whence it came, with the occupants perhaps a trifle dashed in spirit. Drifts began to cross the road, first one, then two, and at length three feet deep. Soon it became impassable. I had hoped I might penetrate as far as Oare Post and enjoy that wonderful prospect over the heart of Exmoor. I persevered for another half-mile, and then had to give it up, for now the snow was over my knees.

Retracing my steps, I met another fellow-creature whose

intrepidity put the two motorists to shame. He had pushed a bicycle, to whose handlebars was attached a bass bag which contained a turkey, up the thousand odd feet from Porlock. And he proposed to traverse some ten more snowy miles to Lynton. I did my best to dissuade him with dismal tales of cars buried in unfathomable depths at Lillycombe and Culbone Stables, and pointed to a darkening sky which looked ominous. But, unpersuaded and indomitable, he decided to continue his trek. Whether he spent the night in a snowdrift, his head pillowed upon the turkey and stags nibbling at his frozen whiskers, I cannot say. If my sanguine traveller ever reached Lynton he deserved to enjoy his Christmas dinner; it was well-earned.

An Admiral's Childhood

JOHN MORESBY

A century earlier, in 1830, a boy was born at Allerford, the next village to Porlock. His father was a naval man, who rose to the rank of admiral. The boy, John Moresby, followed his father's example. He joined the navy at the age of twelve, and also became an admiral, as well as a famous explorer in New Guinea. In 1909 he wrote his autobiography, and his fond

memories of childhood at Allerford included three of the most important Christmas customs still celebrated in nineteenth-century Somerset.

After this diversion [the harvest home feast] the village worked and slept until Christmas brought the high tide and holiday of the year. Anxiously we children listened for the thundering knock at the door which announced the mummers, when, in answer to our scream of 'Who's there?' would come the masculine chorus:

> Here come I, old Father Christmas!
> Christmas or not,
> I hope old Father Christmas
> Will never be forgot.

The bridge and ford across the Horner Water at Allerford

It certainly would not by us. We tore the door open, and in marched a medley of villagers, armed with wooden swords, paper helmets, and ribbons streaming from their smocks – a glorious, jovial sight. Immediately St George stood forth – the majesty of England incarnate – and challenged the Turkish knight to deadly combat, whilst breathless we watched the fight until he fell before St George's conquering sword. There was a pause full of awe for us, and then the victor demanded in the epic strain that befits heroes:

> Is there a doctor that can be found
> To cure this knight of his deadly wound?
> (accentuating the rhymes of 'found' and 'wound').

There was. The doctor, smock-frocked and rosy, stood forth and declared with all the confidence of his profession.

> I'll touch his eyes, his mouth and chin,
> And say, 'Rise, dead man, and fight agin!'

It was done; the resurrection was completed with a few whacking blows, and our feelings were relieved accordingly. Then cider and sixpences followed, and the singing of the old Somerset and Devon ballads – 'Widdicombe Fair' and the like – until, with a final cheer for my parents, the mummers departed to awake the village echoes on their devious way home.

We children had Exmoor ponies, which we rode bare-backed as we galloped over the moors. With a bent pin baited with caddis we landed miraculous catches of minnows, and sometimes even a trout, from the myriad waters of that land of streams. But the Christmas coming of the Aclands at Holnicote was the purple patch of our year. There we all fore-

gathered, young and old, round the wood fire in the hall where on Christmas Eve lay the Yule-log – an ashen faggot bound with seven withy bands – and as each band cracked and snapped in the flame, with clapping of hands and infinite rejoicing we each wished a wish.

Later [generally on Twelfth Night, although Moresby places it in the autumn], as night closed in, the custom, descending from heathen times, of wassailing the apple-trees was faithfully observed. Every old gun, blunderbuss, or pistol that the village could produce was brought out, and masters and men, women and children, all trooped to the principal orchard, the men with their guns, the women with wassail-bowls filled with cider hot and spiced, and bobbing with roasted apples. Then, with shouting and cheering and a general *feu de joie* over the trees, all joined in the chorus:

> Old apple-tree, I wassail thee,
> And well mayst thou bear
> Hats full, caps full, rooms full,
> For cider bright and fair.

Finally, a piece of bread soaked in cider was left on the branches of a tall apple-tree.

The Wassailing Party

F.W. MATHEWS

The mummers, the ashen faggot, and the wassail – all lovingly remembered as essentials of the traditional Somerset Christmas. Because they were so much enjoyed, and made such an impact on young minds, they were often recalled in later life, and a number of descriptions have survived in print. We shall look more closely at each, beginning with the wassail. Admiral Moresby told us nothing about the 'warm-up' for the wassailing party, but that deficiency is amply supplied by F.W. Mathews, in one of his Tales of the Blackdown Borderland, *which were published in 1923.*

The big settle was pushed back from its usual place near the fire, and a sturdy long stool or 'verm' was placed nearly end-to-end with it, alongside a table, on which reposed several large jugs, with their smaller accompaniments of mugs, one-handled and two-handled, and near by a jar of tobacco. Beneath the table stretched several pairs of corduroy covered legs, some lanky, some short, some bandy or bowed, and all presenting a solid array of hob-nailed soles facing the warmth of the ashen 'facket' that blazed on the broad hearth-stone.

The occasion was the wassailing of the apple-trees, but the purpose of this preliminary meeting was to warm up the inner and outer person before going out into the 'Home Orchet' for the observance of the old custom.

'Wull, maester, us be a comed wance moar to wish th' ole Zummerzet tree gude luck. I kin mind thik ole tree zince a was but zoo high,' said an old weazened man, indicating with his sinewy hands and knotted fingers the height of the tree in its younger days.

'Ees, Dan, wance more, and I be sa glad to zee ee all here, looking sa viddy,' replied the old 'maester', his round face beaming under the influence of good fellowship, pleasant memories, a warm fire – and good 'zider'. 'Now, veel up, me gude vullers, gie a rale gude zwig, and let's 'ave a zong or two vore we goes out in the cold. Yu kin gie us wan, cahn'ee, Jan – thik ole lidden about the vuzz-taps.'

'I du most vergit en, maester, but ah'll try what I can du.'

'Yur, yur,' 'That's raight,' 'Goo on, Jan' – from various corners.

A snowy day on the Quantocks, photographed by Iris Hardwick

'Wull, then, wan leedle drap – yurr goos,' and in a lusty voice he trolled forth the following:

> Oh the vuzz he be a blessing ver us all,
> He'm a shelter ver the purty burds to rest;
> And his taps du make a sparkling vire in Vall,
> Oh the vuzz o'bushes all's the vurry best.

> Now the vuzz is all a bloomine on the hill,
> And the vuzz-bush is a gude ole vriend to I;
> Vor e drows his blossoms wi a rare gude will,
> If the saison be a lapprey wan or dry.

> Oh the vuzz du keep a glowin vaace and bright,
> And never lookies dull the whole year droo;
> The vuzz-bank's gold's a glorious cheery zight.
> He smiles the Old Year out and welcomes Noo.

> He du layve off bloomin' so zum voakes du tell,
> When luv and kissin's out o' vashion turned;
> But I've never know'd layve off – never shall!
> Ef du – may all noo-vashioned voak be burned.

Uproarious applause greeted this warm sentiment, and proved the spirit of Marian days not dead, while many an arch approving glance was cast over shoulders at the cheery-cheeked maids who stood behind, alert to attend where the jug or cup seemed to need replenishing.

'Now, Tom, thee cast gie us a zong tu, cassen?' quoth Maester.

'Doan know's I caan, zur, but Aw'll tell 'ee a yarn, ef yu be a-minded.'

'Awright, goo vore.'

'Wull, I went to Tant'n, zom time agone, and when I was

in to Vower Alls, a chap there told I bout ole – no I ont tell his name – ow 'e comed home wan night bit later'n usual, and that wadden very airly nayther.

'His ole dumman ad gone to baid and leff the back door unbolted, so he went in pantry and looked round ver summat tu ait, ver the walk 'ome 'ad made en a bit pickish. Wull, in pantry he found a main gude bowl-vull o' custard and a big spune handy by. He took em in by the vire – there was a bit left in grate – and he zot down and tucked into it, and ait the lot. And he enjoyed it, too. Then he zot a bit longer and smoked a pipe, and valled asleep in chair. Next morning 'e went out and done up the hoss and comed in to breakus. Zoon' he clapped his haid inzide door, his wife said, "Purty goins on agin last night. 'Ave 'ee zeed thik basin I put in cubberd in pantry?"

'"Ees, I 'ave sure, and clained en all up. 'Twas mortal gude custard, too."

'"Custard, yu gurt fule," her scraimed, "custard! Why that was starch, yu drunken toad, and *there was dree yards o' lace ver my petticoat in it*."'

'Ho, ho, ho! Haw, haw, haw!' roared the company at the conclusion of the tale, the initial volley of laughter tailing off into spasmodic bursts and shrieks from one and another as various aspects of the scene tickled the risibilities of the hearers.

'Where du er live tu, dist zay, Tom?' queried one.

'Didden zay at all, and baine gwain to tell,' quoth Tom, 'but I doos a gude laff to mezell every time I passes thik owze when I goes to Tanton market.'

'Thy turn next, Beel, gie us wan of then ole zongs thee grandfather larned thee.'

'Ees, zur, ow'll theaze du – "The Ole Varmer and the Pixymen".'

'Fuss-raet; toon up an' less 'ave thikky-wan.'

With a throat-clearing sip of the 'zider', and a preliminary adjustment of the unaccustomed collar, Bill gave his song, which though rather long, was listened to with great attention by the company, to whom time was of less moment than a tale, and the making out of a good long evening the recognised procedure for such an event as the celebration of Old Twelfth Eve.

'That's a gude un, Beel,' said Maester, 'and a purty long un, too. However dist mind en all? Time's gittin on, I zee,' glancing over at the 'long-sleever' in the corner. 'Come on, boys, light up the lanterns,' and out trooped all the company of men and lads to the orchard.

'Now then, round in a ring,' and they grouped themselves round the oldest tree in the orchard.

The first part of the ceremonial of wassailing was to take a piece of toasted bread and dip it in a mug of cider, then put it up in the fork of the tree. The one who had placed the bread stood back, the oldest member of the company came forward, pointed an old blunderbuss up into the branches and blazed away, while all the others shouted, 'Hip, hip, hooray!' 'Good luck to thee!' and such other appropriate remarks as occurred to them.

Then, the older members of the company leading with the solemnity befitting such a sober ritual, came the old wassail song:

> Wassail, wassail, all round our town,
> Our cup it is white and our ale it is brown;
> Our bowl is made of the good old ash tree,
> So now, my brave fellows, let's drink unto thee.
>> Hatfuls, capfuls, dreebushel bagfuls,
>> And a gurt heap under the stairs.
>> Hip, hip, hurrah (shouted *ad.lib.*)

A wassailing party firing guns through the branches of apple trees
to ward off evil spirits

There was an old man who had an old cow,
And how for to keep her he didn't know how;
So he built up a barn for to keep his cow warm,
And a little more cider won't do us no harm.
   Harm, me boys, harm; harm, me boys, harm;
   A little more cider won't do us no harm.

Down in an old lane there lived an old fox,
And all the day long he sat mopping his chops;
Shall we go and catch him, oh, yes, if we can,
Ten thousand to one if we catch the old man.
   Harm, me boys, harm; harm, me boys, harm;
   A little more cider won't do us no harm.

14

A poor little robin sits up in a tree,
And all the day long so merry sings he;
A widdlin and twiddlin to keep himself warm
And a little more cider won't do us no harm.
　　Harm, me boys, harm; harm, me boys, harm;
　　A little more cider won't do us no harm.

A lady comes round with her silver pin,
Pray open the door, and let us all in;
For this is our 'sail, our jolly Wassail,
And jolly go we to our jolly Wassail.
　　Harm, me boys, harm; harm, me boys, harm;
　　A little more cider won't do us no harm.
　　　　Hurrah, Hurrah (again *ad. lib.*)

The music was as quaint as the words, and the tune was somewhat like the old barrel organ's tune that I once heard played to a hymn in one of the old country churches, in that it fitted the words *sometimes*.

'Zing up boys! A little more zider ont du us no harm,' chimed in old Dan, at the conclusion of the song, a remark which of course evoked much laughter, and the production of the required beverage, brought out piping hot by the thoughtful maids. Sipped to the accompaniment of interjected, 'Good luck, ole apple tree,' it proved very comforting.

A final tipple indoors, with a 'mouthful' of bread and cheese, and the ancient ceremony was over, but for the time-honoured concluding song of old Dan, without which none of the assembly would have considered the evening properly brought to a close.

'Now then, Dan'l, "The Juniper Tree" vore us goes home,' and Dan'l, nothing loth, gave the well-known old song, *The Juniper Tree*.

On the first day of Christmas my true love gave to me
  A part of a juniper tree;
On the second day of Christmas my true love gave to me
  Two turtle doves and a part of a juniper tree.

And so it went, each verse the longer by one line, and all the other lines repeated, till the last time there came the formidable list of:

> Twelve bulls a-blaring,
> 'leven lords a-leaping,
> Ten ladies a-dancing,
> Nine bears a-biting,
> Eight hares a-running,
> Seven swans a-swimming,
> Six geese a-laying,
> Five golden rings,
> Four collie birds,
> Three French hens,
> Two turtle doves,
> And part of a juniper tree.

This memory-taxing catalogue finished, 'Goodnight, Maester; goodnight, Missus,' was the leave-taking, and in the clear night air could be heard for some time, as the various small groups dispersed, the refrain of the old song in different parts of the parish: 'And part of a juniper tree.'

Catching the Words

WALTER RAYMOND

*The West Country wassail fascinated folklorists and
antiquaries around the turn of the century. They were
particularly eager to find parallels in other cultures, and to
suggest that it had pagan antecedents. An important part of
this study was to report how the custom was practised in various
places, and to record the words of the wassailing song. Walter
Raymond, a native of Yeovil, devoted much of his life to the
study of Somerset folklore and traditions, and during the
1890s published several novels of country life, in the genre set
by Thomas Hardy. Here, from* Tryphena in Love, *which
appeared in 1895, we find ourselves in the middle of a jittery
romantic scene between hero and heroine – when there is a
kerfuffle outside.*

'Miss Mervin seemed to take a great fancy to you, John,' she
said, suddenly looking up from the burning logs.

The words startled him. He could not hide his agitation
sufficiently to answer her.

But happily, to his relief, at that moment came the sound
of voices by the porch.

'The Wassailers!' he cried eagerly. 'Now I must get the
words. Find some paper to write them down. Do, Tryphena!
There's a dear.'

The singing began at once.

The black dog o' Langport have a-burned off his tail,
An' this is the night of our jolly Wassail.
  Vor 'tes our Wassail,
  An' 'tes your Wassail,
An' joy be to you, vor 'tes our Wassail.

'Quick, Tryphena; have you got it? Quick.'

Wassail! Wassail! all roun' about town,
The cup it is white, the ale it is brown;
  Vor 'tes our Wassail,
  An' 'tes your Wassail,
An' joy be to you, vor 'tes our Wassail.

The cup is a-made o' the merry ashen tree;
The beer is a-brewed o' the best barley,
  Vor 'tes our Wassail,
  An' 'tes your Wassail,
An' joy be to you, vor 'tes our Wassail.

'You will have to do it when they come in, Tryphena. I
would not miss getting the words for anything,' he said, his
voice trembling with anxiety.

Missus an' Measter a-zitten by the vire,
An' we poor travellers a-traipsen drough the mire,
  Vor 'tes our Wassail,
  An' 'tes your Wassail,
An' joy be to you, vor 'tes our Wassail.

Missus an' Measter be you zo well a-pleased
To zet 'pon your table-board the white loaf an' cheese,
  Vor 'tes our Wassail,
  An' 'tes your Wassail,
An' joy be to you, vor 'tes our Wassail.

Kilve Abbey in the snow, a painting by W.W. Wheatley, 1847

Maid, perty maid, wi' the little zilver tag
Now do ee urn to door an' show your perty lag,
   Vor 'tes our Wassail,
   An' 'tes your Wassail,
An' joy be to you, vor 'tes our Wassail.

'Nip down to door, Tryphena. I suppose they mus' come in. They'll be ill-pleased else,' cried Mrs Pettigrew from the foot of the stairs in an unwilling tone of discontent. She regarded such songs and rites as obsolete, but it was bad judgement to offend the labouring folk. John, thinking only of the verses, wistfully watched the girl depart.

Maid, perty maid, wi' the perty zilver lace
Now do ee come to door an' show your perty face,

> Vor 'tes our Wassail,
>   An' 'tes your Wassail,
> An' joy be to you, vor 'tes our Wassail.

'I won't have 'em go upstairs, Tryphena,' added Mrs Pettigrew sharply. 'They'll bring in all too much dirt as 'tes.'

> Maid, perty maid, wi' the little silver pin,
> Then do ee ope the door an' let us all in,
>   Vor 'tes our Wassail,
>   An' 'tes your Wassail,
> An' joy be to you, vor 'tes our Wassail.

He heard the door open and the clatter of their hob-nailed boots upon the kitchen floor. Then he waited, listening intently to catch Tryphena's voice inquiring about the words. But he could hear nothing clearly above the noise and din of the whole company. And at last, before departing, they sang again:

> Missus an' Measter, now we mus' be a-gwain,
> But do ee ope the door when we do come again,
>   Vor 'tes our Wassail,
>   An' 'tes your Wassail,
> An' joy be to you, vor 'tes our Wassail.

Some little time elapsed before Tryphena returned and quietly resumed her seat. 'I've got most of it,' she said, 'and old Abe is coming in tomorrow.'

'You dear,' he cried enthusiastically.

But Tryphena did not respond as formerly, and for a while she was silent. Then gazing into the fire, she began to build her castle in the air. 'Miss Mervin told me what a lot she thought of your saying the poetry, John,' she began. . .

A Peculiar Witchery

WALTER RAYMOND

Let us stay with Walter Raymond for a little longer. Another of his novels, Young Sam and Sabina, *which was published in 1894, includes inimitable descriptions, not only of the wassail ceremony itself, but also of burning the ashen faggot beforehand.*

There they all were. Happy souls! of the days before hospitality went away by rail.

'Come on! Zit down! Now then, Missus, where's thik bit o' supper?' cried the farmer, in a voice boisterous enough to raise the roof.

A singular angularity of elbows and knees, which marks the earliest period of a rural festivity, vanishes under the genial influence of good cheer. A roast turkey invites contemplation and affords food for thought. A ham, well cured, is an inspiration, particularly if there still lingers in the mind a recollection of the pig to which it once belonged; and cousin John Priddle had known that pig from its earliest infancy. It puts a man at ease to sit down with an old acquaintance. Every tongue was loosened; every heart was gay; and when supper was finished they drew around for the great carousal.

'Come on! All draw up! Now then, Missus, make haste wi' the cup.'

''Tes a wonderful girt fakket, sure enough,' chirped Christopher.

'Ay, ay! Wi' a extra bind to please Widow Sharman.'

'He'll make the women-volk hop more 'an once, I'll warrant un!' cried cousin John Priddle, rubbing his hands.

'Zo he will. Now then, Missus, dap down the cup 'pon the settle close handy like. Put back the chimbley-crooks. Move out, Sabina. Now then, soce, let's heave un on!'

So the great ashen faggot was lifted upon the hearth, and the eager flames leapt up around it, licking with their red tongues the hazel binds.

Now the glory of the ashen faggot was this. When a bind burst, sometimes with a mighty crack, casting bright sparks

'The Cider Drinkers', a woodcut by Claire Leighton, published in 1934

and splinters out into the room, and the women shrieked and pushed back their chairs, and the men threw back their heads and laughed, – then, and not until then, the cup was handed round, and everybody drank his best without loss of time, so that it might be drained and filled again before the next explosion.

'I never didn' zee a better fakket, not in all my life,' exulted Christopher.

'I think the vire have a-got hold o' un now,' shouted the farmer, taking up the cup, and resting it upon his knee in readiness.

'Look out! Look out!' cried cousin John Priddle, and Widow Sharman nervously raised her apron to cover her face.

It was a false alarm. The faggot went on burning without any sense of responsibility, just as if the discomfort of thirst and the blessing of cider had ceased to exist.

'Put the cup down avore the vire, Zam. Else he'll get cold,' nervously suggested Mrs Grinter.

'I never didn' zee a fakket hold together so long in all my life,' suggested cousin John Priddle, in considerable anxiety.

'I sim myself, 'tes a funny thing,' agreed Christopher, stroking his bald head to promote thought.

''Tes,' said the widow.

'Zo 'tes,' chimed in Mrs Grinter, with an unusually anxious expression on her little sharp face. 'An' eet o'cou'se, it can't be another. Pick up the cup, Zam. He'll get so hot else we shan't be able to hold un to our lips.'

'I'll be dalled if I shan't want bastin' soon. I be so dry as chips,' moaned Christopher.

'Here, push out measter's little voot-stool, Sabina. Dap down the cup 'pon he. Little bit closer. No, not too close. Zo.'

Farmer Grinter drew the back of his hand across his forehead. 'Do make I puff an' blow,' he said, and sighed at the delay.

'I'll be daazed,' whispered cousin John Priddle, 'if I don't think they bands be witched.'

A fearful solemnity fell upon that party, as if everyone were afraid to speak; and, although the flames were now rushing high up the chimney-back, all stared into the glowing mass and quite forgot their thirst. One by one the binds melted away like wax. As Christopher afterwards protested with suspicious emphasis, they were all 'to a miz-maze like,' and he broke out all over into a most terrible sweat.

The startled voice of Sabina first broke the silence.

'Massy 'pon us! Why, there be chains in the vire.'

'What?' yelled old Sam Grinter, leaping to his feet, making not only the women hop, but Christopher and cousin John Priddle as well. 'Then, so sure's the light, somebody have a-got at my fakket. Dash my wig and burn my feathers! if they didn' chain thik there poor fakket up under they halsen withes so as he couldn' bust. An' we all a-zot round like jackass-vools. That's gwaine beyon' a joke. I don't zee no joke in that.'

'I do call it ignorance,' said cousin John Priddle.

''Tes.' 'Zo 'tes.' 'An' that 'tes,' chorused the ladies.

Just a glimmer of mischief, or was it only a fancy of the firelight, flickered upon Christopher's little round face, and then he said quite quickly, extending his hand for the cup –

'But if they thought to keep Sophia from drinking, they'll be main-well a-sucked in.'

That was the way they always joked Sophia, but she only took the cup, and smiled, and sipped.

The moon was well up and joviality completely restored by the time they were ready to wassail the apple-trees.

'Come on, then! Come on! Have 'ee got your guns?' cried the farmer, as, still clutching the cup, he led the way across the mow-barton, weird with mysterious shadows from the stacks, and into the little dark orchard behind the homestead.

The women-folk had thrown shawls over their heads, and on they all went, laughing, stumbling over the leaning trunks in the uncertain light, and sometimes running into the boughs, on their way to the old Jack Horner tree in the corner.

The ceremony was simple, but impressive. The farmer had brought the sodden toasts from the evening's carousals, and now placed them in the 'vork' of the tree. Then the company repeated the ancient formula:

> Apple-tree, apple-tree
> I do wassail thee
>   To blow an' to bear
> Cap-vulls an' hat-vulls an' dree bushel-bag-vulls
> An' my pockets vull, too.

Toasting the apple trees with cider

Then they cheered and fired their guns, with such infinite success that even Christopher's old flintlock went off – after a brief interval. And thus, please God, was an admirable crop ensured, and the proceedings came to an end.

Yet not quite to an end. There is a peculiar witchery about the moonlight glancing between apple-trees. It seems to dance and sparkle upon the branches, and yet in the shadow the ground is as black as night. It has a confusing effect upon the brain. A feeling of fantastic unreality as of a ubiquitous will-o'-the-wisp creeps over the imagination, and even Solomon in all his glory might easily lose his way.

They all lost their ways.

The unanimity of Middleney suffered a slight shock on the question of the situation of Church Farm, for Mrs Grinter saw the orchard gate, distinctly and with considerable asperity, in two opposite directions.

Sabina knew she was right, and said so with a self-reliance which carried conviction – at least as far as Ashford was concerned.

So they found themselves apart.

'Look there, Mr Ashford!'

'What is it? Where?'

The girl's arm was raised, pointing to a branch overhanging their heads upon which grew a thick mass glistening in the moonlight.

He stood staring with all his might; but, before he could recognize the mistletoe, with a burst of laughter she had flitted away among the trees.

Here Comes I. . .

Although all mumming plays share common elements and the same theme of death and rebirth, there seems to have been an infinite variety of details. Just as with the wassailing songs, Somerset folklorists have been concerned to preserve the 'scripts' of as many as possible, in so far as a set dialogue was adhered to by the performers. Now enjoying a revival, mumming plays, like folk singers, were regarded as moribund at the beginning of this century, and so they were collected and published by enthusiasts as a matter of urgency. But the mumming play which follows was written down much earlier, a few years after 1800 in fact, and it is quite a curio. Not only was it circulated in print as a broadside (by Nott, a Taunton printer), but it also mixes up with the traditional elements various subjects of national pride, such as contemporary battles (Trafalgar and Quebec), and guest appearances from real and imaginary heroes and villains. The result is an unusually high casualty rate, and a grand confusion of miscellaneous characters in search of a story line.

OLD FATHER CHRISTMAS, Or a New Play for the
Christmas Holidays.

First: Open the door of the room in which the company
are, and begin with the following words:
Open the doors, and let us come in,
I hope your favours we shall win;
Whether we rise, or whether we fall,
We shall do our endeavours to please you all.
The merry time of Christmas is now drawing near;

I wish your pockets full of money, and your cellars full of
  beer,
And if you'll not believe what I do say,
Walk in, Old Father Christmas, and boldly clear the way.

Old Father Christmas
Here comes I, Old Father Christmas, welcome or welcome
  not,
I hope old Father Christmas will never be forgot;
Altho' I am come, I have but a short time to stay,
'Twas I, that led the King of Egypt away.
Room! Room! give a little room to sport;
For in this house I mean for to resort,
For to resort and merrily to play;
Walk in, the King of Egypt, and boldly clear the way.

King of Egypt
Here comes I, the King of Egypt, as plainly doth appear,
St George is my only son and heir.
Walk in, St George, and boldly act thy part,
That all this jovial company may see thy noble art.

St George
Here comes I, St George, that did from England spring,
Some of my mighty works for to begin.
First in a closet I was kept,
From thence into a cabinet,
From thence upon a rock of stone,
There did I make my sad and dismal moan,
Whilst many men did strive me to subdue,
I ran my firy dagger through and through;
I fought them all courageously,
And still came off with victory.
For England's right, for England's admiration,

Here I draw my bloody weapon with vexation.
Where is the man will me withstand?
Let him come in, and I will cut him down with my
    courageous hand.

Prince Valentine
Here comes I, Prince Valentine, so fair a man renown'd;
Soon shall thy haughty courage tumble down,
As for a fall thou shalt receive of me,
So let us fight it out most manfully.
Hold, hold, St George, let us shake hands before we fight;
Thou first challeng'd me, I next challenge thee,
So let us fight it out most manfully.

*(St George and Prince Valentine now fight, and, after some
struggling, Prince Valentine is killed; but while he is lying on the
floor, Prince Amoric, his father, enters and says:)*

Prince Amoric
As I was arising out of my bed,
I heard my only son was dead.
O cursed, cursed Christian! What hast thou done?
Thou hast ruin'd me, by killing my only son.

St George
He did me the challenge give. How could I him deny?
You know how high he was, but look how low he lies.

Prince Amoric
O help me, help me, Sambo! for never was there greater
    need.
Wilt thou stand idle, with thy sword in hand?
Come and fight, like a loyal subject, under my command.

I see him there dead, which makes my heart
To bleed. Distracted shall I run;
So I'll lie down, and die by my only son.

(Prince Amoric lies down by the side of Valentine, and dies.)

Sambo
Prince Amoric's law will I obey;
With my sword and spear I hope to win the day;
For yonder is he that spilt my master's blood,
And with his body will I make an ocean flood.

St George
O doctor! is there ne'er a doctor to be found,
Can cure these champions of their deep and deadly
  wounds?

Doctor
Yes, yes, St George, there is a doctor to be found,
Can cure these champions of their deadly wounds.

St George
What is thy fee?

Doctor
Ten pounds is my fee; five only will I take of thee.

St George
Where hast thou travelled?

Doctor
France, Italy, Germany, and Spain.

St George
What canst thou cure?

Doctor
The itch, palsy, and the gout,
All pains within, and pains without,
And if the devil is within, soon I'll fetch him out.
I have a little bottle in my pocket, call'd Virtue and Fame.
Here, Jack, take a little of my flip-flap, put it into thy tip-
    tap;
Rise, Jack Slash, and fight again.

(Prince Valentine and Prince Amoric now gets [sic] *to life again,
and rising, says:)*

Prince Valentine
O terrible! terrible! Was like ever seen,
That men should be brought from their seven senses into
    seventeen?

Bloody Warrior
Here comes I, a Bloody Warrior, spent all my time in
    bloody wars,
And now I'm return'd, cover'd with wounds and scars.
I've serv'd King George both by land and by sea,
And now I'm content in Old England to stay;
But of all the battles that I have fought on my way,
Was the glorious battle in Trafalgar's Bay;
And as I'm return'd, in Old England to dwell,
I'll drink to the heroes who on that day fell.

Admiral Nelson
Drums, beat to arms!
Trumpets, sound to Fame!

I am a British hero,
And Nelson is my name.
Remember, on the 21st of October,
That being the very day,
Nineteen sail of the line,
Some we took, and some we sunk,
And some cowardly bore away.

Admiral Duncan
Drums, beat to arms!
Trumpets, sound to Fame!
I am a British hero,
Admiral Duncan is my name.

Benefit performances of a comedy
and a melodrama in Crewkerne
Town Hall on New Year's Eve,
1819

General Wolfe
Drums, beat to arms!
Trumpets, sound to Fame!
I am a British hero,
General Wolfe is my name.
I have scaled many rocks,
And climbed many walls;
Neither was I haunted nor daunted at all,
Till a bullet struck me on the gall.
As I lay bleeding on the wat'ry sands,
I heard a voice say 'Bear up, General Wolfe, and die in my
  hands'.

Little Man John
Here comes I, a little man, John Slasher is my name;
With sword and buckler by my side, I hope to win the
  game.

St George
I am St George, that man of courage bold,
And with my sword and spear have won three tons of gold.
I slew the Dragon, and brought him to the slaughter,
And by that means I won the King of Egypt's daughter.

Turkish Knight
Here comes I, the Turkish Knight,
Come from the Turkish land to fight,
To fight St George, that man of courage bold,
Altho' his blood be hot, I soon will make it cold.

St George
Hold, hold, proud Turk! pray don't you be so hot,
For in this room is one thou knowest not;
Here is one that will cut thee as small as the dust,

And send thee to the devil, to make apple-pie crust;
I'll cut thee and slash thee as small as the flies,
And send thee to the devil, to make mince-pies;
I'll cut thee and slash thee, and after I've done,
I'll fight the bravest champion under the sun.

Turkish Knight
You first the challenge gave, and I the challenge took,
And why should I of you refuse a stroke?
Draw out thy sword and fight, draw out thy purse and pay,
For satisfaction I will have before I go away.

St George
No satisfaction shalt thou from me have,
For in one moment I'll make thee an English slave.

(Here St George and the Turkish Knight fight.)

Turkish Knight (being wounded by St George, says:)
O! hold thy hand, St George; for one thing of thee I crave;
Spare but my life, and I will be thy slave.

St George
Get thee home unto thy Turkish land,
And tell what noble champions in England stand;
Ten thousand of such ones as thee I'll fight,
For to maintain the Crown of England's right.

Turkish Knight
Here I arise and go away;
God bless King George, and all his ships at sea.

Tom Bowling
Jolly sailor, jolly sailor, Tom Bowling is my name;

Here's me and men, and men like war,
Just come on shore, in hopes to beat eleven score.
We'll set our guns aboard of them,
We'll make a dreadful noise,
We'll make the King jump off his throne,
And all the people shout for joy.

Fire Poul
Here comes young Fire Poul, as you may understand;
Walk in, young Crumell, and take me by the hand.

Young Crumell
Here comes I, young Crumell, as you may plainly see;
I think, young Fire Poul, I'm man enough for thee.

St George
I am St George, and the battle soon will try;
He that is resolv'd to fight, come, fight with me and die.

Last: Gentlemen and Ladies,
You see the Turkish Knight is to be conveyed to the Castle;
Let your voices thro' this room ring,
And be so well pleased as to put something into our
  Christmas Caps, and say,

God save the King.

Mrs Comfort's Party

If mumming plays are one of the forms of entertainment on offer
during the run-up to Christmas, here is another, to be enjoyed
by the participants and endured by the adults. Cast your mind
back to schooldays – do you remember the school end-of-term
Christmas party? In 1927 Lewisham School, a rather genteel
establishment for boys in Landemann Circus, Weston super
Mare, held two Christmas parties, under the supervision of the
headmaster and his wife, Mr and Mrs Comfort. This one,
reported subsequently in the school magazine, was for boys
under twelve, and must have been typical of hundreds of similar
celebrations.

Friday, December 17th, was the date chosen by Mrs Comfort
to hold her Junior Party – only boys under twelve years of age
being invited.

As the hall clock chimed six, small boys in Eton collars and
Sunday suits were to be seen shyly wending their way to the
drawing room, where Mrs Comfort was waiting to receive
them.

Previously a number of small objects had been cleverly
hidden about the room, so each boy was provided with a
pencil and card on which to write the names of the things he
found. After searching carefully for about ten minutes the
small competitors were seen to be anxiously comparing their
number of successes, another five minutes and all the cards
were collected and given to Mr Comfort for correction.

Later on, games were played in the dining hall. It was great
fun to see the boys trying to balance themselves in a basket

hung on a brush handle resting on two chairs. They were given a stick with which to steady themselves sufficiently to knock off the pennies on the chairs without overbalancing. This looked an easy task and many a boy confidently waited his turn – but, alas! he shared the fate of his predecessors! 'Basket on top, boy underneath!'

If one can judge by the amount of laughing and singing which accompanied the game of 'Musical Chairs', it certainly should be voted one of the favourites of the evening. As the number of players decreased so the excitement increased, until at last only two boys were left – then another few bars of music, which suddenly stopped, left the proud victor seated on the remaining chair.

Various other games were played until eight o'clock, when supper was served in the library. Seven of the tallest boys were chosen by Mr Comfort to help him look after the ladies and younger guests.

The supper table was very artistically arranged. In the centre, surrounded by gaily lighted candles, was a tall trifle shaped like a tower, containing a variety of charms. After justice had been paid to sandwiches, sausage-rolls, mince pies, cakes and jellies, the trifle was served. For a while everyone was very quiet, then there was a general chorus of, 'Look what I've found!' or, 'I've found a lucky shoe!' or, 'Here's Pip, Squeak or Wilfred!'

When supper was over the boys returned to the drawing room, where Mrs Comfort distributed small prizes to the winners of the different games. The lights were then turned out and the room was transformed into a veritable Fairy-land by the stars that showered from the 'sparklets' held by the boys.

The ringing of the front door bell announced the arrival of parents and friends, so after the boys had said goodnight to Mrs Comfort, and thanked her for such a pleasant evening, the party broke up.

The Week before Christmas

H. HAY WILSON

*Another way of passing the time as the festive season approaches
is to bring out and dust down the old tall stories, of the
'Haven't I ever told you the one about. . .' variety. Here is such
a tale, thick with dialect, which might have circulated in the
pubs of the Pensford area a hundred years ago. Like all the best
Christmas stories, a ghost is involved.*

'Here be Doris feared to go whoam alone. Boys have been a
tellin' her pack o' lies about the ghost to Parsonage Lane.'
Doris's rosy face was tearstained and pale when Mary Andrews
looked at her, rather awe-stricken.

'My dear lamb,' she said, 'thou shouldst mind Them as do
guard thee, and not fear what thou canst not understand.'

'Now, Mary, you be foolish,' said John impatiently. 'Why
don't 'ee tell the maid right out as there be'nt no such things
as ghosteses, and they gurt loobies should hev' a swap behind
the ear for trying to frighten little maids. Run along, my dear,
and goos wi' uncle Jem, he'm gwain home-along just now.'
And Doris trotted away after her uncle.

'Policeman do say he do know thiccy ghost,' John went on
angrily, '—'tis naught but a gurt ivy-bush do stand high up
pitching forward in hedge above Weaver's trap where the road
do fall by the water-gout. He do stand up there above the
rexen so dark, and pleeceman say he do often vancy 'tis

Varmer a standing there by gate, and do look up to speak to'n, and 'tis but the ivy-bush. And there be'nt no other ghost there, not as he do know by.'

Granfer Dyer was of another opinion. 'There'm more sights abroad than what us do always know,' said he, taking his pipe out and looking at John. 'And Weaver's Fatherlaw could have told 'ee better, for he did know my Veyther. Hevn't I a' told 'ee o' the zight my Feyther did see over to Park at Christmas time?'

John snorted, but said no more, because Granfer Dyer's story was an institution in the village.

'It were the week before Christmas,' said the old man, 'and my Veyther he were a terr'ble one for the Methodies, and he'd a-druv over to a meetin' to Bristol, and were coming back late, past Rectory and down by Five Gates, where 'ee know there'm a old road do come out that did used to be the old ancient way for all travellers before roadses were made proper. An' there'm an bit of him do come out all alone by himself in middle o' Park field, where they fir-trees do make a lew place for cattle, and do look still as if had been a bit o' old road as somebody had forgotten about. It were a regular mirky night wi' clouds heavy above, an' Veyther said 'a could see the lights of Bristol a'glowen in sky low down as it med be a furnace, gurt ways off, an' a big smeech o' cloud hangen over 'en, as do when rain be gathering, an' the sight o' thiccy glow did make Veyther think on the gurt vire as Parson do talk on, where the wicked go. It mid a been thic Methody chap he just a-heard did zet Veyther's thoughts like that, but he were a wonderful religious man, were Veyther, tho' 'piniated, an' did fetch all o' we hard over the head wi' gurt Book when us didn't versy right, Zundays. An' he were so sober a man as walked, and never a bit market-fresh.

'Well, there were Veyther wi' Hell-fire in's head which weren't a convanient thing to zet 'en home by of a dark night,

Icicles at Adscombe on the Quantocks

but he would hev' knowed the way blind-mobbed, and so did old mare. Well, he were come so far's Five Gates, where old road do come out 'way past they Knaps like gurt emmetbuts where bones do lie buried, and 'ee do know 'tis tur'ble lonesome. Veyther he did zwer' around for to go down Hen Lane, an' 'tis so narrow's a want-wriggle, an' dark, one do seem buried like a carvy-zeed in a cake down there o' nights. So Veyther did cast a look over's shoulder to see there weren't nothin' behind 'en as shouldn't be there, for they lights in sky did zim to run in's head, and after he did turn away from they

did seem like the darkness held 'en round so tight's a cheese-wring. 'Tes mirky there when do fall night. Sure enough he did see summat, an' that were a two-double pair o' lighteses behind 'en, as it mid be of a gentleman's carriage, tho' Veyther did know gentry don't often go by there unless they'm miswent. An' 'tweren't old Squire neither for Veyther did know as he hed took sick an' wer' bad a-bed, and volk dedn' look to see 'en last the year out. An' it were the week before Christmas. Well, Veyther were frightened to see quality that way, but it ded'n scare 'en nowise, an' the lights were martal bright. But he did vind a quare thing, and that was, tho' night were so still 'ee could hev' heard a berry dapping in the hedge, yet a' couden' hear a pat o' the harses' hoofs, nor yet a sound o' wheels, and road be riddly down to they knaps.

'Well, a diden' think so much o' that, and old mare were getting on at a tidy pace, when something did make Veyther twirdle hisself round on seat to look behind, and there, if they lighteses hadn't turned into Hen Lane too an' were coming along fast behind 'en, an' now he did hear the harses' hoofs a'trampling fast and nigh to 'en. 'My dear life,' thinks Veyther, 'however shall we get'n passed.' For the lane be that strait two carts can't pass, nor yet hardly a rave-waggon get along. Now, Veyther haden' the bad manners to be keepin' back quality behind 'en, so he did fetch the old mare a whack, as weren't used to that from he, and her did fling up her heels and set off at a pace. An' Veyther look round again, and see they lighteses gettin' nearer and hear harses a tramplin' and gallopin' like the wind, so he did whoop to they to keep back till could pass, but they didn' heed 'en and came on gallopin' like the wind. They did get so near, Veyther could see four harses an' a big coach, real magnifical, behind 'en, an' that scared 'en a bit for there weren't such in they parts. An' 'a could see mimmickin' vellows in tight breeches an' high

boots a' sittin' on harses' backs, an' the tails o' the leaders did swish across 'en an' 'pear to dout the flame for a two-three seconds, and then did glimmer out again a-swinging to the gallopin' of the harses. But the back-lamps of the carriage did shine steady like the flame of a gurt cat's eye in the dark. Veyther he dedn' like the 'pearance of'n, an', thinks he, they'll surely run we down, though the mare did vlee as if she had Old Vengeance at her tail. So Veyther did see they were nigh upon Summerlease by Wapsill's gate, where there'm a passing place and road be wide for maybe two acres and a ben. Now, they'll can pass, thinks Veyther, an' good riddance. So he did zwer' aside to let 'en pass. An' old mare wooden' stop, yet the pace they harses were a'gwain were nigh twice so fast as her. So Veyther couden' believe's eyes when did look back an' see coach weren't the leastest bit nigher, an' they harses a' gallopin' like the wind. So did try to pull up old mare, but she were ugly after the blow, an' wouden' bide still.

'Well, thinks Veyther, at Forty Acre they'm bound to pass we, an' when they got past Bloody Paddock, where Forty Acre do lie after the garden spot, Veyther did put all his heft on reins and pulled old mare on to grass wi' her nose over gate, so's her couden' get no farther, bein' too witty a beast to try an' climb. An' there her stood a' sweatin' and a' heustering while Veyther were glad to think they'm bound to pass now. He did look around, and they so close, could see the steam rise on harses' flanks and dim the light behind, and there were they unchristian lanterns o' the riding-boys a'dancing wi' the harses stride, an' the tails o' the leader a' douting them every minute, an' harses all the while a' gallopin' like the wind. They wer' so close as I be to you, or most near, an' 'ee do know, there'm a road do turn out by Bloody Paddock an' run along towards Tip. And 'tis hill-land there by, and all moory where water be ponded, and the road so rough wi' all the ravvle o' the quar'. An' top of 'en, the tip o' redding stuff do

stand nigh to little wood that Parson do say be part of old road of ancient days.

'Now just when Veyther did think they would be past 'en, come the moon a'ridin' out from behind a cloud, and did shine sudden so bright as had been high-by-day, and he did look round for the coach, and would you believe 'en, thic coach dedn' niver pass Veyther, for while he did look around the four harses did zwer' an' dash down by thic little narrow old way like a rabbit down a wriggle an' – "Massy a' me," think Veyther, "sure they'm zogged an' stooded," for he couldn' hear the tramplin' nor the wheeels a' rolling no more. He stood there up in cart, did say, as he med hev' been a pillar o' salt, wi's head twirdled round over's shoulder, an' mouth open so wide's a bat could hev' flown in at 'en. At last he did think to pull mare's head round an' set her home again, and her by now so quiet's a christened babby.

'So he turned about, and when did look up towards top (the

A winter scene on Exmoor

moon were gone in by then) there were lights a' flashing far off to other end of the lane nigh to Manor House, and they were going slow and stiff towards Tip, and there'm a gate by there, thou knows, do lead up to Tip, but 'tis always barred when miners be gone home. But Veyther could see from below, coach did dash through gate place just so fast as had galloped down road, an' they queer lanterns a' jumping and swinging, and the leader's tails a' swishing across them. They did head straight for the wood, a' gallopin' like the wind, and when they reached the lew place, that were the last Veyther saw o' the lights, for they went out, 'a said, in the night like a candle flame a' blown out, an' the dark did shut down over 'en like a sack over a live coal.

'Veyther, he did stand in a maze, an' the old mare too, when sudden he did hear steps, and there was a man coming in front of 'en, after the hedge an' going fast, tho' as if he were a bit catching. When did get near, Veyther see it were P'liceman Pascoe, an' him a' pankin' like a ewe in a thunderstorm – he were a stout man – an' his face so white's milk, as Veyther could see by's one lamp. "Where be gwain, Pleeceman?" Veyther axed of 'en, but Pleeceman didn' answer, and Veyther were scared to see 'en, knowing 'en to be so valiant a man as walked, though not too well liked on account of his never drinkin' wi' nobody. But he'd fear no man's face nor yet not a company. Well Pleeceman Pascoe did grip old mare's bit as if he were glad of the feel of her, and pank – he were a stout man – so Veyther did ax of 'en after a bit would he get up an' hev' a lift. Pleeceman did get up beside Veyther and sit there an hicker as if he were cold. And when they did get whoam to house, Pleeceman purled on's feet as did get down, and Veyther axed of 'en to come in an' sit down, "for I'm feared," says he, "you've had a turn." Wi' that Pleeceman turn to Veyther, and 'a says, – "Mr Dyer," he says, "you know I be a sober man." "Why, for sure," says Veyther, "an' some don't like 'ee the better for it," he says,

meanin' to comfort 'en like. "Well," says Pleeceman, looking a
bit pearter, "I'll tell 'ee what come to I this night, an' the first
night ever I didn' knaw if the world were real about me."

"'It were up to Manor House," he said, "to end of Long
Walk, where wall be almost ruinous, and there'm a little
thatchen summer-house like a hay-pook in the moor of a gurt
beech. Well, Squire's gardiner did 'quaint I last night as some
shark had been round to poultry yard and had boned seven
pullets, and 'tweren't a fox for was footmarks. So I think –
here'm a rare place to climb in by – for 'ee know, old Squire be
such a hunks he woulden' niver mend's fences." Well, end o' it
were Policeman Pascoe did clamber through fence, careful like
– he were a stout man – and did peek wi's lantern inside
summer-house to see if were anyone there. An' just then what
do 'a hear but steps a' coming along Long Walk, gurt ways off,
near to house. So Pleeceman, he thinks, "I'll catch the villain,"
'a says, an' did step inside summer-house so slick's a weasel an'
did quat down amid scroff and twigs within. There were a gurt
brack where haps were off door, and 'a could look drough, and
all were so still, 'a could hear a bird peat in the rexen. The
steps did keep a' comin' nigher so slow he could tell 'en one by
one, and, thinks he, "'a'll soon be nigh." Then moon did come
out sudden and so bright as 'twere high-by-day, and Pleeceman
could count every mop o' grass on path, and, thinks he, "'tis
lucky I did get inside while 'twere dark, an' the villain cann't
hike off nowise." An' still the steps kept coming nigher. An'
just when they did turn corner there were Pleeceman feeling so
sprack's a cat over a mouse, biding still wi's eye at the brack.
An' steps come louder, and slower, an' yet slower, an' did go,
slow, right a' past the door of the summer-house all in the
moonlight, an' there were Pascoe a' lookin' right upon 'en as
did pass by an' – eh, my dear life, there were nothing there and
nobody at all in sight, and yet they footsteps did stop, and pass
on, an' go away in the moonlight, though there weren't

nobody there, says Pleeceman, his voice going up in a sob like a sick child's.

'Veyther said 'a did feel the flesh fair creep upon's bones when did look to Pascoe's face an' see it all wet wi' the terror of what he hadn' seen, an' just then they did hear harses' feet come clatterin' up to the house in the night. An' 'twer' the gardener from the Manor to say how old Squire had died in a fit sitting in's great chair an' looking so grim as he did when did turn his son out o' doors, and would Veyther ride wi' 'en for doctor, for he were feared to go alone in the dark. So they all dree did go, for none o' 'en woulden' be left alone wi' the terror o' what he'd seen in's head. An' it were the week before Christmas, an' there were still thiccy glow in the sky did make Veyther think all the while o' the gurt flame where the wicked do go.'

Granfer stooped to relight his pipe and looked across at John on his couch rolling sightless eyes at him in the darkness. ''Tis a wholesome thought for the most of us,' said John.

Muscatels in Clusters

The week before Christmas can easily strike terror into the stoutest of hearts — but not so much because of the ghosts, rather because of the last-minute shopping. It is the time of year when shopkeepers try the hard sell, enticing their panicking customers

with irresistible delights. So it seems now, but so it was also a hundred years ago – as this selection of advertisements from Weston newspapers demonstrates.

CHRISTMAS NOVELTIES. Cosaques! Cosaques! Cosaques! An immense and choice selection, from 5d to 5s per box. Fancy boxes of Chocolates and Metz Fruits, from 3d to 21s. A large stock of Fancy Tins of Biscuits, and Iced Cakes, including Banquet, Chatsworth, Almond Iced, Richmond, Festival, etc. etc. Muscatels in clusters, or layers, from 10d per lb. Carlsbad, Elva, and French Plums. Finest Stilton, Gorgonzola, Camembert, and Cheddar Cheese. An early inspection is respectfully invited. Price list on application. CLARKE & NORMAN, 18 REGENT STREET, WESTON SUPER MARE

The Mayor of Bridgwater, accompanied by Father Christmas, distributes toys to children in the Town Hall

Christmas 1894. CHARLES WIGMORE, Fruiterer and Potato Salesman, 23 Meadow Street, Weston super Mare. In returning Thanks to his numerous Customers for their past Patronage and Support, begs to say that he has a good supply of English and Foreign Fruit, and all kinds of New Nuts, reliable for Christmas use; also a large assortment of First Class Potatoes, namely Schoolmasters, Beauty of Hebron, Magnum Bonum, Bruce, etc., and of the finest quality, which cannot fail to give entire satisfaction. English-fed Turkeys, Geese, Chicken and Ducks at lowest possible prices. An inspection respectfully solicited. Note the address: 23 MEADOW STREET, WESTON SUPER WARE

Xmas 1894. Useful presents. Ladies in search of useful articles for presents should call and see WM. C. THOMAS'S Stock, which is now replete with an immense variety of articles suitable to the occasion, at Popular Prices. Ladies' Fancy Aprons, Servants' Aprons, Pinafores, Servants' Caps, Silk Squares and Mufflers, Lace Fronts and Collarettes, Purses, Fans, Handkerchiefs, Handkerchiefs in Fancy Boxes, Wool Wraps, Gloves of every description, Hosiery, Umbrellas, Jackets, Capes, Mantles, Silk Blouses, Skirts, Fur Boas, Collars and Muffs, Millinery, Mob Caps, Dress Lengths, Cosies, Cushions, Antimacassars, Curtains, Table Covers, Down Quilts, etc. etc. 4 HIGH STREET, WESTON SUPER MARE

Buy your Christmas Presents at SYDENHAM & SONS, Furnishing and General Ironmongers, Brass Pole Makers, Plumbers, Gasfitters, etc. Special discount of 3s in the £ off all Lamps during this month only. See our Special Carpet Sweeper, manufactured expressly for Christmas Presents. No advance in price. 5 MAGDALA

BUILDINGS (Three doors from Shaftesbury Hotel), WESTON SUPER MARE.

Christmas 1894, at the WESTON BAZAAR.
 Who has not heard of the Weston Bazaar?
 Or seen the delightfully dazzling display?
 The choicest collections that come from afar
 Of home manufactures a gorgeous array!
 Of many ingenious and novel inventions
 To charm young and old at the time of 'Good Cheer'.
 Our choice is so large that the closest attention
 To what we may briefly enumerate here,
 Is not half so good as a casual inspection,
 A gentle walk round to behold our display;
 There's no entrance fee and we make no collection,
 In fact our friends tell us we give things away;
 All the most popular games of the day,
 All that's alluring, instructive, or pleasant.
 Charming the serious, amusing the gay;
 Suited alike to the peer or the peasant,
 Spoof Anno Mundi, Go Bang Cannonade,
 Flitterkins, Ludo, Reverie, Glissade,
 Chess for the serious, Snap for the jolly,
 Pliffkins for Harry, Patcheel for Polly.
 If undecided just send for a list,
 A chance like the present should never be missed.
 Boxes of puzzles for those who desire
 To seek entertainment at home by the fire.
 Boxes of cubes, Architectural bricks,
 All that is novel in Conjuring Tricks;
 Dolly's own Mail Cart and Dolly's delight,
 Dolls with three faces, with two and with one,
 Dolly's that cry in their terrible plight,
 After they're purchased they soon may have none.

As for our varied assortment of Cards
Christmas and New Year, they tell us our show
Is quite unapproached in the town, as regards
Their beauty, and that's saying much as you know.
MORAL: If you would please, you had better by far
Take all the dear children to Coulsting's Bazaar.
Rocking Horses, Mail Carts, Bicycle Horses, Doll's
Houses, and all the large and useful Toys in immense
variety at the WESTON BAZAAR, 24 HIGH STREET. Look
at our show in the windows opposite, No.73, and then
come and walk round the Bazaar.

The First Christmas Card

Blame for the pandemonium of Christmas shopping can be laid
squarely, and on the highest authority, at the door of the three
supposedly wise men who came from the east bearing gifts. But
who is responsible for the scramble to meet the deadline of the
latest posting date for Christmas? Who invented the Christmas
card? There is nothing in the Biblical story about sending cards
– indeed without postage stamps and letter boxes, to say
nothing of printing, cardboard and envelopes, the commercial
Christmas card is a difficult concept. But Somerset historians

have always maintained that it was a wise man from the west, a native of Bath, who first had the idea.

Sir Henry Cole was an affable, bewhiskered Victorian gentleman who died in 1882 with a splendid string of achievements attached to his name. He had helped to set up the Public Record Office, to introduce postage stamps, and to organize the Great Exhibition of 1851; he founded the South Kensington museums, raised the money to build the Royal Albert Hall, and initiated what became the Royal College of Music. In his spare time he learnt etching, published illustrated books for children, won a prize for designing a tea service, and fathered three sons and five daughters. And in retirement he organized a cookery school, and was a director of a company which reprocessed sewage. Bath, where he was born in 1808 (the son of a dragoon

Sir Henry Cole, inventor of the Christmas card

guards captain and his wife), should feel proud to have produced such a man.

Oh yes, and he invented the Christmas card. His autobiography, which was issued soon after his death, devotes only one line to the fact, with an illustration, and a footnote explaining that by the 1880s more than twelve million extra items of post were being sent each Christmas week, with a stamp value of £58,000. The first of Cole's cards, issued in 1846 (according to the caption in his memoirs), has three illustrations. Its centrepiece depicts a benign wine-drinking paterfamilias amid a tableful of children and other relatives, and he is flanked by smaller pictures of the hungry being fed and the naked being clothed. The design was drawn for him by an artist, John Calcott Horsley, and a thousand copies were issued for sale as part of his children's magazine venture, under his pseudonym Felix Summerly.

Modest though they are, Somerset people have from time to time ventured into print to claim this 'first' for their county. For example, in the *Somerset County Herald* in January 1904 Sir Henry Cole's first card, of 1846, was described, along with the observation that it was not until 1862, sixteen years later, that commercially produced cards came into general circulation, with designs of holly, mistletoe and robins.

Twenty-one years after this newspaper entry, in 1925, the matter was re-opened. A correspondent who styled himself 'SANTA CLAUS' (so he does exist, after all!) wrote in to ask:

> I have heard it said that the custom of sending Christmas cards originated in Somerset, and that the first cards of the kind ever known were made by a Somerset man less than 100 years ago! I find it difficult to believe this, and should be glad if you or any of your readers could tell me if there is any truth in this story – SANTA CLAUS.

Santa, via the *Somerset County Herald*, received four letters in reply – others may have been stuffed up the chimney, of course. Two reiterated Sir Henry's claim, and a third noted that the early Christmas cards had been disliked by his extremely evangelical family as being a high-church product of the Oxford Movement. But the most interesting reply came from the redoubtable Willis Watson of Crewkerne.

I have always been under the impression that the Christmas card originated at Bath, and that the names of J.C. Horsley, RA, and Sir Henry Cole were associated with it. And I had written a reply to Santa Claus to this effect. Within a few minutes of completing my task the post brought me the *Newcastle Weekly Chronicle* for Saturday December 19th. A notes and queries column is a feature of this paper, and, naturally, I always turn to this. Judge my surprise when I noticed the heading of the first note was 'The First Christmas Card'. What a strange coincidence – the very words I had myself written but a few minutes before! [Perhaps Santa had dropped a line to the Newcastle paper as well.] I read the note in the *Chronicle*, and I destroyed the one I had intended for the *Herald*. If the *Chronicle* correspondent is correct, Somerset can no longer claim to be the birthplace of the Christmas card. I am wondering whether Newcastle can either, because, after all, with the art of printing invented in the fifteenth century, it would be risky to assert that no member of the craft during the period 1471 to 1845 printed a message of goodwill to his nearest friends at Yuletide, and even included an illustration by way of a wood-cut. Here is what E. Wells says in the *Newcastle Chronicle*.

'Christmas cards, which have regained much of their old

popularity, were first printed in Newcastle. In 1845, the Rev Edward Bradley, known as a writer as "Cuthbert Bede", sent designs for Christmas cards to Mr Lambert, the well-known publisher and stationer at Newcastle, and they were printed for private circulation. This was repeated in 1846, and in the following year the printers conceived the idea of putting designs on the market. In 1847–8 they offered the cards for sale, and these were the first cards offered to the public. This origin of Christmas cards was vouched for by Mr Thomas Smith, who in 1845 was Messrs Lambert's foreman printer, and who, soon afterwards, started in business on his own account.'

It will be noticed that the Newcastle cards were not publicly sold until 1847–8 [Willis Watson continues], so Somerset beats Newcastle by a year on this point. The Newcastle cards could not have been the first cards offered to the public, because it is not quite reasonable to think that Sir Henry Cole would have had 1,000 cards printed in 1846 for private circulation. But at present, it seems as if the honour of designing the first card belongs to Edward Bradley, as his is dated 1845, three years before he took his BA degree in University College, Durham, and when he was at the age of eighteen years.

So Somerset honour was satisfied, but only by a whisker. And there the matter seemed to rest until January 1935, when 'H.C.' (perhaps one of Santa's mischievous relatives?) wrote to the *Somerset County Herald* with exactly the same inquiry. This time a new threat emerged. The then current issue of *The Stamp Lover*, as 'READER' pointed out, included a reproduction of the earliest known Christmas card. It was by a sixteen-year-old boy, W.M. Egley, and it was dated – horror! –

1842. Worse still, as 'F.F.' elaborated in his reply to the newspaper, Egley was born in Doncaster; and there was another hat in the ring, too. In 1844 W.A. Dobson, Queen Victoria's favourite painter, and a native of Germany although of English parentage, painted a card and sent it to friends instead of his usual Christmas letter. But all these contenders – Egley's and Dobson's, and Bradley's too – 'F.F.' dismissed as 'a purely private affair'. Cole's, however, was the real thing, and 'it may therefore be said that as a commercial proposition Christmas cards owe their inception to a Somerset man'.

Yes, that was Willis Watson's patriotic verdict, too. He had not been idle in the cause of Somerset's vindication since the previous threat. He had apparently found a letter published in the *Times* in January 1882 (in fact it was 2nd January 1884). It was from a Joseph Cundall of Surbiton Hill:

> The first Christmas card ever published was issued by me in the usual way in the year 1846 at the office of *Felix Summerley's Home Treasury*, at 12 Old Bond Street. Mr Henry Cole (afterwards Sir Henry) originated the idea. The drawing was made by J.C. Horsley, RA; it was printed in lithography by Mr Jobbins, of Warwick Court, Holborn, and coloured by hand. Many copies were sold, but possibly not more than 1,000. It was the usual size of a lady's card.

So perhaps Willis Watson had trumped his opponents and won the trick for Somerset. But he still had misgivings. After rehearsing the contents of his 1925 reply he ended with a question: 'If anyone has access to Sir Henry Cole's autobiography, perhaps some reference to Christmas cards could be found and decisive evidence forthcoming that the Christmas card really had its birth in Somerset.' And indeed it does – in a way. The card was issued, its caption maintains, in

The first Christmas card

1846, but the footnote mentioned earlier ends by claiming that it was designed in 1845. A misprint, perhaps? The plot thickens.

What none of our heroic Somerset correspondents knew was that the battle they were fighting had already been won, many years earlier. First the artist Horsley, as an old man in 1883, had written to the *Times* explaining that, although he had designed and drawn the first Christmas card, it was entirely Sir Henry Cole's idea. And then it had been left to Sir Henry's daughter, Henrietta Cole, to strike the opposition a fatal blow. In November 1903 she wrote to *Notes and Queries*:

> . . . I may say that I have in my possession one of these cards, coloured, and sent by Mr Horsley to my father, with the inscription 'Xmasse 1843', three years earlier

than the first issue of the cards; and, wishing to verify the date, I consulted my father's diaries, and found the following entry: '17th November, 1843, Mr Horsley came and brought design for Christmas card'.

She was quite right. By the time that a definitive history of the Christmas card came to be written, in 1954, several examples of the card bearing the date 1843 had come to light. So that had put paid to Dobson's claim (1844), and to Bradley's (1845). Only the boy-artist W.M. Egley (1842) was still in the running. And even his supporters had to admit that the 2 in 1842 was cramped – it could be an 8, or even a 9. That matter had been settled in 1935, when a Mr H.J. Deane wrote to the *Sunday Times*. He possessed one of Egley's cards, and Egley himself had written on the back, 'Christmas Card – the Second ever published. Designed and etched by W. Maw Egley, 1848, India proof'. So Egley himself, perhaps anticipating this barrage from scribbling antiquarians, had already conceded defeat. And now it is Sir Henry Cole, the native of Bath, who appears proudly each year in the *Guinness Book of Records* as the man responsible for the first Christmas card – which, as we now know, was sent out in 1843. And don't let anyone try to persuade you otherwise!

Christmas at the Post Office

A great man, no doubt, but Sir Henry Cole was not perhaps the most popular customer when he nipped into the post office to send his Christmas cards. Every Christmas his invention led to frantic scenes, and every Christmas local newspapers carried reports of the heroic exploits of postal staff. We visited the shops in Weston super Mare a century ago – now let's call in at the post office (courtesy of a somewhat verbose Weston Mercury *reporter).*

Shades of Gibbons! Shades of Matthews! Less than forty years ago the whole of the business at the Weston super Mare Post Office was not only conducted but carried out by the late Miss Gibbons, she being the only recognized Government Post Office clerk for this district in those days, whilst the duty of delivering such missives as persons residing at a distance from time to time forwarded to their limited acquaintance at Weston super Mare was undertaken by Her Majesty's solitary representative in that department, who was better known as 'Jemmy', as a prefix to the surname of Matthews, than by any other designation.

Less than forty years have passed away since those worthy officials were in sole charge of Her Majesty's mail in our midst, and what do we find at the present day? Why, a staff of over sixty men and boys engaged in connection with the Weston super Mare Post Office, including a postmaster, a sub-master, fifteen clerks, thirty postmen, nine telegraph messengers, and a whole host of supernumeraries for exceptional work.

The season of Christmas is one when the services of these latter are especially called into requisition, and the calling up of these 'reserves' no doubt materially strengthened the standing army in their attack on, and subsequent defeat of, the foe, in the form of an overwhelming mass of correspondence. The seven days prior to the week immediately preceding Christmas Day chanced to be the 'out season count-out', the information obtained by such counting being forwarded to St Martin's-le-Grand, so that headquarters may ascertain the amount of work despatched by our local postal force: to ascertain that there are not included on the staff other than real working-bees with plenty of work to do, and so decide that none are too liberally paid by the so-called 'Working Men's Government' of the present day. The 'count' referred to showed that during the week over 63,000 letters and newspapers – to say nothing of parcels – were received and delivered in Weston super Mare, and that within the same interval over 58,000 documents of a similar character were despatched. These figures will give some slight idea of the work carried on at our Post Office 'out of the season'; to the extent to which such work is increased when Weston is 'in season' we will leave our readers to imagine.

But it is more with regard to the Christmas season that we have now to speak, and we are reliably informed that during the week preceding Christmas Day, the work at the Post Office – both in the receiving and despatching departments – was fully five times the ordinary average; or, in other words, 315,000 letters received and delivered, and 290,000 despatched. In the *Pirates of Penzance* we are reminded in song and verse that, 'a policeman's life [*sic*] is not a happy one': what shall be said of the Post Office officials, at a season of the year when the greater number of the community are on pleasure bent? It is at this festive season that the officials in our great state-managed business are hard at work sorting and preparing for delivery the thousands and millions of missives which on Christmas morn are

to bear the message of 'Peace on earth, goodwill toward men'. Let us hope that, as a slight acknowledgement of the valuable services rendered by the civil, obliging, and by no means over-paid servants of Her Majesty, that the 'postman's knock' will remind householders that they have a social duty to perform.

The laborious duties of the clerks may be imagined when we state that on Christmas Eve at the General Post Office no less than £76 worth of stamps were retailed. On Christmas morning the delivery at Weston super Mare commenced at 10.30, when each regular employee was allowed a 'super' to carry the heavy baggage – in fact, a biped luggage van – and with his assistance the whole of the heterogeneous mass which had arrived by the night mails was successfully distributed to those entitled to receive them shortly before two o'clock in the afternoon – the mass in question comprising about 80,000 letters and parcels. The work of the department in Weston super Mare was greatly facilitated by the prevalence of mild weather, which enabled the mail carts to arrive and depart with punctuality, whilst with regard to the train service there was little to complain of as compared with some previous years – the greatest delay being under one-and-a-half hours.

The actual posting of letters for the merry season was late, which was attributed to Sunday coming before the Eve of Christmas, and during the whole of the 24th letters were poured in in shoals so long as the office remained open. With the assistance of four supplementary stampers the whole of the 'receipts and disbursements' were successfully dealt with, and the damaged consignments are next to nothing. Letters and Christmas cards bearing such a vague address as 'From Frank to Percy' failed to find the persons for whom they were intended, but these instances were few and far between, whilst some singular addresses were readily deciphered by those accustomed to the work, or several would have been minus a practical remembrancer of the season.

The new Post Office – the site for which in the centre of High Street has been acquired for nearly two years – not being in a sufficiently advanced state to be designated 'the receipt of custom' for the parcel post department, a large room opposite the present contracted premises was again utilized, and so relieved the congestion which would otherwise have occurred at the Post Office proper. The average business in this department is about 1,900 parcels per day received, and 1,400 transmitted. During the five days preceding Christmas 5,600 parcels were received, containing, for the most part, game, geese, turkeys and plum puddings. The whole of these practical reminders of the season were delivered in good time, and in each instance, we venture to imagine that to the recipients, the 'postman's knock' was the most musical tone that had previously been heard this year.

A Withered Rose

ALICE KING

Somewhere among the thousands of jumbled packets and envelopes in the 1894 Christmas rush must have been copies of the latest issue of the Argosy, *one of the many magazines with which Victorian families whiled away their leisure time. The December issue carried the last contribution by a Somerset writer, Alice King, who had recently died. It was an account of*

*her life, spent at Cutcombe on Exmoor. A remarkable life it had
been, too, since Alice had been blind from early childhood.
Nevertheless she rode the moors on an Exmoor pony, taught
herself to use a typewriter, was a tireless and inspiring teacher
in her village, played the guitar, and wrote novels and poetry,
as well as occasional pieces for magazines such as the* Argosy.
Her December contribution to another magazine, Home
Chimes, *three years earlier had been a Christmas story, and
here is part of it.*

First of all, let us step into the old grey village church; the
door is open, for the ancient sexton is doing what he calls
'putting up the Chrismassing'. The December twilight comes
on apace, and the whole building is unpleasantly suggestive of
ghosts, but the old man says quite cheerfully, 'If there be any

Cutcombe Church, a painting by W.W. Wheatley, 1849

spurrits here, I ban't gallied at them,' and he puts on a jaunty, not to say familiar air, as he talks of such spectral visitants. For all head-gear he wears a red handkerchief curiously knotted and arranged around his head and face, and he looks very much as if one of the gurgoyles round the tower has just come to life and stepped down from its usual elevated situation.

The hand of the architectural restorer has not yet touched this church; the high pews are like so many commodious loose boxes for captured Exmoor ponies to take their ease in; the east wall is pierced with a quaint little square window, and above the pulpit there is a strange, canopy-like erection, called a sounding-board. There is no want of Christmas decoration, albeit of no aesthetical and artistic style. The church looks as if a small neighbouring plantation of evergreens had just walked into it. Old Mat, as they call him in the village, has 'put up his Chrismassing' to a purpose; from every corner and cranny blooms forth a branch, even from the half-broken hand of the crusader who lies on the monument in the southern aisle. Scarlet berries are hanging in rich profusion; though they are twined into no elegant wreath, they climb up to the centre arch, where is displayed that curious old picture of Moses and Aaron, Mat's joy and pride; they fringe the front of the gallery, where tomorrow the Christmas anthem will ring out with a will from clarionet and bassoon, without any weak assistance from St Cecilia and her organ-pipes. That Christmas anthem will be, in truth, a wonderful and unique production in the musical way. How will the choir roll forth the prolonged notes, how will the melody wind in and out and twist itself into marvellous turns and trills, how will the words return again and again until the heads of the listeners will almost be giddy with the complex evolutions of sounds. The faces, too, of the Christmas choir will be a study worthy of a Rembrandt in their solemn, absorbed, ecstatic enjoyment of their own music. Old Mat

will lead the strain, and he will be sure to be equal to the occasion; he and his fathers before him have sung that Christmas anthem, for it is impossible to say how many years, and generation after generation in the church have listened to it in rapt admiration.

But let us leave the church and old Mat, and, guided by the Christmas moon of frosted silver, pass up the deep lane, where the mosses are still green even in mid-winter, and turn into the roomy, rambling old farmhouse. Through the large porch we go, with the curious deep niches on either side, made, it is said, to accommodate the immeasurably long clay pipes called in the West Country 'churchwardens'. The pipes used to rest in these niches when the smokers removed them from their mouths awhile. A little fountain of sweetly chirping girlish laughter ripples down towards us from the wide oak staircase as we enter the hall; the girls are tripping from room to room ornamenting their beds with holly. If a West-Country maiden sleeps on Christmas Eve on a bed unadorned with a holly spray, she is quite certain to be visited with all manner of evil spirits and goblins to punish her for her omission of the time-honoured sacred rite.

But why is sweet Bessie, the farmer's dark-eyed daughter, absent from her merry companions? She is sitting in yonder deep window-seat, where the moonbeams are falling softly on something she holds in her hand, while her cheeks burn and her heart beats. Let us steal across the room, and take one glance at that object, which she touches almost reverently as her fingers lightly close over it. It is a withered rose. For some time Bessie has loved handsome Robin, the young Exmoor farmer, whose uncle is her father's neighbour, and there seems some reason to believe, by certain signs and tokens known in the silent alphabet of lovers, that her affection is returned. But Robin is a very shy wooer, and Bessie, like all West-Country girls, is very proud and reserved, and the courtship therefore languishes.

Thus is has come to pass that Bessie has hit upon an exceedingly original way of making her backward suitor declare himself. Long ago, in the bright summer time, she gathered a blush rose on Midsummer day, and stealthily, secretly, so that not even her mother could know, she laid it by carefully in the inmost recesses of her drawer. She has thought of that rose all through the golden harvest weather, and dreamed of it at night, and now, on Christmas Eve, she has taken it out from its hiding-place, and tomorrow she will go to church with the withered rose in her breast. Robin is

A scion of the Holy Thorn, photographed at Brent Knoll by Iris Hardwick in January 1972

paying a Christmas visit to his uncle, and Bessie fully believes that if in reality he loves her, he will be compelled by the virtue of that charmed, withered Midsummer rose, to go up to her when he meets her on Christmas morning, and take it from her bosom, and this will be an infallible sign that his heart is hers, and they will be married before another Christmas day comes round.

We have left sweet Bessie now dreaming still in the moonlight, and are sitting in the settle of the farm kitchen, a most snug and inviting place on a cold winter's evening. The fire, which burns on the hearth without any grate, but flanked by two old-fashioned fire-dogs, sends forth a ruddy glow; the huge brass warming-pan, the most precious and cherished treasure of the farmer's wife, for it was a treasure in her family even in her great-grandmother's time, shines like burnished gold as the blaze dances upon it. The chimney-piece is as broad as a Chinaman's umbrella.

And now the most important West-Country custom, indispensable on Christmas Eve in every properly constituted West-Country farmhouse, is at hand. The door of the kitchen is opened wide, and the oldest labourer on the farm walks majestically in, carrying a huge ashen faggot on his shoulders. No West-Country farmer would have any good luck throughout the coming year if the ashen faggot was not duly burned in his house on Christmas Eve. The faggot — which is a goodly load of wood, such as might be a respectable burden for a Spanish mule crossing the Sierras — is set on fire with much pomp and circumstance in the broad hearth; there is a furious crackling and snapping of the branches, and a roaring of the blaze up the wide chimney, such as might reasonably arouse uncomfortable fears in a nervous guest, and the Christmas family bonfire is burnt with peals of riotous laughter, and merry jests, and brisk volleys of fun, among young and old, master and men, mistress and maids, together.

The most favourite amusement of the young people in the West Country is dancing. They are as fond of it as the French peasantry when they dance at the festivals of their chosen village saint. These West-Country dances are always danced around the Christmas ashen faggot. As we sit in the settle corner, we mark with pleased eyes the natural, untaught grace of the girls as they weave in and out through the often complicated figures of the strange, old-fashioned West-Country dances. There is one dance, called the 'Handkerchief Dance', which is a perfect silent poem, as the girls with their partners – fine stalwart young fellows, whose limbs have been knit together and braced by many an Exmoor breeze – pass and repass, and raise their arms, and sink almost on their knees alternately, and form themselves into a changeful, living web of movement, ever recurring, and yet not one moment the same.

Among the elder folk there is much handing round of 'cobler's punch', a West-Country mixture of cider and gin, and much singing of songs. These songs are many of them very quaint as to words; the two most characteristic, perhaps, are a song, the chorus of which imitates all the noises made by the different animals on a farm, the whole party going into the performance when the chorus comes round with right good heart and will; and a song which glorifies the good qualities and useful properties of the horned Exmoor sheep. The songs are interspersed with Christmas carols, some of which are very ancient and curious, and the music of which has never probably been printed, but lives in the minds and hearts of the people alone, re-echoing on from Christmas to Christmas, backward and backward, until, as we strain our ears to catch the sounds, they are at length lost in the murmur of the waves of time.

Songs Ancient and Curious

Taking our cue from Alice King, the blind observer of Exmoor
life, it is time to explore the world of Somerset Christmas songs
and carols. Pride of place must go to a small piece of parchment
found among the Bridgwater borough archives. It is a deed, and
concerns the lease of property in west Wales in 1471; but soon
after it was created (to judge by the handwriting) someone jotted
down on the back the words of two carols, one for Doomsday and
the other for Christmas. They are in English, with a few words
in Latin; between the two, and at the end, the writer has added
repeatedly the words 'holy' and 'yffy' – 'holly' and 'ivy'.

Hay hay take good hede wat you say
a doumsday we schull y see
Fader & sone in trinite
w't grete power and magisti
and angelys in grete aray

And angele w't a trumpat shall blow
that all the worlde schall yt yknow
they that beyne an yyrth soo low
they schull a ryse all off the clay

They that byne in soo deppe
they schull to thys trumpat take heed
And a ryse and full sorre wyppe
that ever they wer to yenst to say

God hymselffe suner hyt ys
that schall ene the dome I wys
And therfore owys hym th't hath I do amys
Fore ther they schull rehersse here pay

Holy holy holy holy holy yffy yffy

Letabundus exultet fidelys chorus alleluia
[Let the joyful chorus of believers rejoice, alleluia]

gaudeamus [let us rejoice]
now well may we myrthys make
For Jhu mankynd hath take
Of a mayden w'toutyn make [husband]

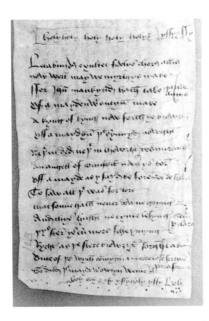

A medieval Christmas carol,
preserved among the
Bridgwater Borough Archives

res miranda [a thing of wonder]
A kyng of kyngs now forth ys browgth
Off a maydyn th't synnyd nowght
Nether in ded nether in thowgth

sol de stella [a sun of a star]
An angell of counsell now ys bor'
Off a mayde as y sayd be fore
To saw all th't was for lore

semper clara [ever shining]
that sonne hath never downe goyng
And thys lyght no tyme lesyng
This ster' ys evermore scheyinyng

para forma [of the same nature]
Ryght as the stere browght forght a beme
Oute of the wych comyyth a marvelose streme
So dud th't mayde w'towtyn weme'

Holy holy & yffy yffy holy yffy Holi

Next is the song which Alice King probably had in mind – the one in which the chorus imitates farmyard animals. This description was printed in a local newspaper in 1922.

The following simple composition, made up on similar lines to 'The House that Jack Built', is known to have been chanted with great gusto at many of these old-fashioned parties. Like that of the man with a tin whistle along a street kerb, the music consisted of 'variations', and just followed the inspirations of the party, whilst, where necessary, the natural cries of the birds and animals were interpreted in the best possible spirit by old and young.

I bought a cock and the cock pleased me, I set my cock all under a tree, my cock went cock-a-doodleloo, and joy to all the neighbours' cocks, and well done my cock, too.

I bought a hen and the hen pleased me, I set my hen all under a tree, the hen went chit-a-chaff, chit-a-chaff, the cock went cock-a-doodleloo, and joy to all the neighbours' cocks, and well done my cock, too.

I bought a duck and the duck pleased me, I set my duck all under a tree, the duck went quit-a-quaff, quit-a-quaff, the hen went chit-a-chaff, the cock went cock-a-doodleloo, and joy to all the neighbours' cocks, and well done my cock, too.

Then follow in a similar manner, the additions of a goose, with her toosee-toosee; a cat, meow-meow; dog, bow-wow; sheep, baa-baa; horse, neigh-neigh; cow, moo-moo; turkey, gobble-gobble; donkey hee-haw, hee-haw; and the bird, sweet-sweet.

By the time the bird begins to sing probably several members of the company have failing memories of the order of the purchases, which generally results in a hilarious jumble up of the various calls of the creatures concerned, and the switching off to some other Christmas game and amusement.

And here is an old Christmas carol from Frome, preserved on a fading sheet of paper in the Somerset Record Office. It is of the 'Green Grow the Rushes' construction.

What shall us sing?
Sing all over one.
What was one?
One was God, the righteous man.
Save our souls, the next, Amen.

What shall us sing?
Sing all over two.
What was two?

Two was the Jewry,
One was God, the righteous man.
Save our souls, Amen.

etc. introducing the following in turn:

Three was the Trinity. . .
Four was our Lady's bow'r [?]. . .
Five was the dead-alive. . .
Six was the crucifix. . .
Seven was the lump of leaven. . .
Eight was the crooked-straight. . .
Nine was the water-wine. . .
Ten was the golden pen. . .
Eleven was the gate of heaven. . .
Twelve was the ring of bells. . .

*Next we remember one of the best of village poets and song composers,
Thomas Shoel, who lived in poverty at Montacute around the
beginning of the nineteenth century. His career was commemorated by
Llewelyn Powys in one of his* Somerset Essays, *and here is an
extract describing Shoel's Christmas music, followed by an example of
Shoel's work. The poem is an allegorical piece, never straying far from
the story of the Nativity, nor from Shoel's own rough experience of
life.*

Thomas Shoel published three books of sacred music: *Ode for
Christmas Day, The Chearful Psalmodist*, and *Peace*; also
innumerable Psalm tunes, hymn tunes, and 'Easy Anthems'.
The best known of all his religious tunes is perhaps his *Joy to
the World*, which when I was a boy was regularly sung by the
carol singers at Christmas. There used at that time to live at
Montacute an old man named Samuel Geard, a lusty
member of the church choir. The family of Geard had seen

better days. Samuel Geard's own father had been a prosperous sailcloth manufacturer. He, however, had been content to earn his bread without cark or care as an under-gardener at Montacute House. On a certain Christmas midnight when the Borough, as the village square at Montacute is called, was white with a fine nativity snow, and a bitter wintry wind was huffling against the sloping roofs from the north-east, Geard heard the carol singers begin to strike up with the 'old tunes'. In a moment he was out of bed, and opening wide the casement window, stood in his nightgown exposed to the shrewd 'draughts', joining with his magnificent bass voice in the 'Shepherd's music' as heartily as the best of the carol singers. His friends called up to him not to risk his life in such a foolish manner. 'I can't bide in bed when you be out singing Wold Tom Shayell,' came back the obstinate answer. (The local pronunciation of the name Shoel was Shayell and not Shoel.) In those days they used to make a great deal of carol singing, the orchestra that accompanied consisting of clarinet, flute, fiddles, and bass viol, and I have been told it was the custom of the cellist to go to the churchyard and tune his strings to the tone of one of the six bells – perhaps to the one which has, 'He that heareth me to sound, Let him alwaies praies the Lord,' engraved about its wide rim.

> Cold was the air, the wind blew strong,
> And darkling grew the evening sky;
> When pass'd a beggar-man along
> And wish'd a friendly shelter nigh.
>
> His coat was rent, his feet were bare,
> And slow he crippled o'er the stones;
> Through his torn hat high stared his hair,
> And shrivell'd skin disclos'd his bones.

Montacute Square, painted by W.W. Wheatley, 1848

With hands benum'd and stiff with cold,
Close folded on his troubled breast;
The weather-beaten wretch behold!
And let your sorrows guess the rest.

Ah! has he left his native plain
To seek employment far abroad,
But work unable to obtain,
Is toiling back his homeward road?

Behold him pass the Public door,
And cast in vain a wistful eye,
For Inns do not receive the poor,
Whose pockets can't their wants supply.

A Somerset Christmas

Now to a stall behold him lie,
Glad with the ox a bed to share;
But poorly cover'd from the sky
And shiver'd by the piercing air.

Good natur'd hind! O don't deny
A shelter in your master's shed;
O grant some straw that he may lie,
A little warm for such a bed.

Come gentle sleep, and let thy hand
Find out the beggar where he lies;
O let thy care-deceiving wand,
Seal for a while the sufferers' eyes.

In vain I wish – the downy power
Flies from the thorny bed of care,
Indignant at misfortune's hour,
And frighted far by stern despair.

His haggard eyes he fain would close,
But ah! his dear distressful train
Rush on his thoughts with all their woes,
And near to frenzy drive his brain.

*Thomas Shoel is seldom remembered today, in spite of the obvious
poetic qualities of his work. As a writer he stands out from the crowd
of would-be local poets who clutter the library shelf. Here, by way of
contrast, is a much more typical Christmas effort, which probably has
not seen the light of day since it was penned in 1901 by W. W.
Butler, a master at Brynmelyn School, Weston super Mare, for the
school magazine. It is headed 'An Xmas Carol'. (Surely a
schoolmaster should have known better.)*

A Somerset Christmas

The Earth has donned her garb of Winter's white;
Two weary Bards tramp slowly o'er the snow;
Though cold the wind, and chill the frosty night,
They sing this cheerful Carol as they go –

Give me the home where the Yule log burns
Heaped high on its ample hearth;
The home to which the wanderer turns
By many a varied path.

The home where friends meet once again,
Whose friendships never tire;
Where tales are told whose ghosts remain
Around the Christmas fire.

While pealing bells proclaim to all,
As merrily they chime,
The happy days our minds recall,
A good old Christmas time.

Give me the hearth where the Yule logs burn,
Piled blazing side by side;
The hearth to which our hearts must turn
To keep the Christmastide.

*Finally, in this sheaf of Christmas songs, is one from Taunton,
collected by the doyen of Somerset folklorists, Ruth Tongue. She
heard it in 1906, and believed it might be a version of a
traditional carol, 'The Holly Boy and the Ivy Girl', used as a
processional dance.*

O the ivy O, she'd grow, she'd grow
And the holly he is white
And the little birds sing because it is spring

And the plough boys follow the plough.
O 'tis ivy O, green ivy O
O the ivy she do grow.

O the ivy O, she do twine all about
And the holly he is green
And they tosses the hay in the field all day
And the sun he do shine out
O the ivy O, green ivy O
O the ivy she do twine all about.

O the ivy O, at the Allern tide
And the holly he is yellow
There be apples fell adown and they picks 'n from the
ground
And they lays 'n in tallat side to side
O 'tis ivy O, green ivy O
O the ivy at Allern tide.

O the ivy O, she is Queen of old
And the holly he is red
Hang'n high on the farm and us wont come to no harm
Till the Chrissimass Days be told
O 'tis ivy O, green ivy O
O the ivy she is Queen of old.

Not Like the Old Days

W.G. WILLIS WATSON

No Christmas celebration is complete without somebody reminiscing about how it used to be, and how Christmas has changed for the worse. We do it, of course, in response to what we see as ever more expensive and sophisticated presents, or greater commercialization, or exploitation, and we think that we are saying something original. But the truth is that fondly recalling the Christmases of our childhood is as much a tradition as anything else. And to prove it, here is an example written before most of us were born. In 1919 a Crewkerne man, Willis Watson, contributed each week to his local newspaper, the Somerset County Herald, *a calendar of Somerset customs, superstitions and folklore day by day through the year. When he came to Christmas Day he indulged in a little nostalgia.*

Christmas Day! What memories it recalls – the bells ringing in the church tower before morning had well dawned, the bursting stockings hanging at the foot of the bed which Santa Claus had stuffed to bursting point during the night, the Christmas cards bringing old friends nearer to one at the very threshold of the great festival; the 'Happy Christmas' from father and mother, brothers and sisters, the red holly and the pearly berried mistletoe, the decorated church and the singing of the Christmas hymns, the turkey at the head of the dinner table, the plum pudding flying the Union Jack, the games

78

afterwards, the iced cake at tea on which was perched Robin Redbreast, then more games, another look at the presents, followed by snap-dragon, then the loving 'Good-night', the snow-white bed, and sweet sleep.

What happy Christmas Days were those we youngsters in our dear old Somerset enjoyed years ago. They are not the same today; they cannot be. The wheels of time have travelled on and change has succeeded change. The things which gave the greatest possible delight to the children of years ago would be scorned by the superior children of today. But are the latter any happier? Are they as happy as when they made their own enjoyments, made their own Christmas decorations, when mothers made their own Christmas puddings, when father made the arrangement by which the Christmas tree revolved?

This latter incident has recalled to my wife, sitting by my side, a real native of Somerset, the Christmas parties of her youth, some fifty years ago, when she and the other members of the family regularly visited a fine old Tudor farmhouse in the neighbourhood of Chard. Here resided a good farmer and his wife and family – a son and a daughter. They, too, were of the Somerset breed – with hearts as true as gold, full of hospitality, and especially happy when others were also happy. Theirs was a lovely old home, with mullioned windows, and a great water wheel at the side used to drive the mill.

The children were fetched in a dog-cart, and on arrival were warmly welcomed. What a dinner was provided – real old-fashioned fare of roast goose and Christmas pudding. The great kitchen was gaily decorated with holly, mistletoe, and evergreens. Then, later on, they wended their way to the dining hall to revel in the delights of the Christmas tree. The youngest member of the party drew aside a hanging curtain very slowly, and what a sight met their gaze! There was a great Christmas tree, lighted by coloured candles. From the

branches depended the most beautiful articles. Hours had been spent in its decoration. There were little figures of Father Christmas, old men and women and children, dangling at the end of elastic, bobbed, and winked at the merry youngsters, as if to welcome them, silver and gold tinsel made the little parcels which contained the most delightful prizes sparkle in the light, and as the tree revolved a veritable fairy scene met the view of the children. Their wonder found expression in various ways, and shouts of delight volleyed and thundered around the walls of the room upon which days had been spent in making it a veritable Christmas picture.

For weeks the good hostess and her friends had been busily engaged in threading holly berries, which now formed all kinds of designs and spelt out words of seasonable welcome. The excitement of the youngsters increased when the time came for stripping the tree. Bags containing numbers corresponding with numbers attached to the articles on the tree were passed round, and each little visitor drew one. What prizes were won amid shouts of delight! All had as many as they could carry. One little maid received from the tree a robin standing on a log of wood, and inside the log was a bottle of scent. She loves robins to this day; another a cloth hedgehog, with its back stuck full of pins; yet another, an egg on a rustic stand, from underneath which a mouse was peeping; others had boxes of bricks. A gun fell to the lot of a bonny boy, and 'thousands of cats' he shot with it in the days which followed. What a chatter, what laughter, what joy. These were happy days.

Then there were games of forfeits, crackers were exploded, and the little ones adorned their pretty little selves with aprons, caps, and jewellery, which were found in the innermost recesses of the crackers. And how lovely were the sugared almonds; there are none like them today. And how the little figures danced on the glass covering the large

musical box. Everyone was merry, the hostess perhaps most of all, for she was delighted when entertaining children. Then tea, then games, then oranges and muscatels, everything to make their young hearts glad. And Father Christmas looked down at them from the top of the tree and veritably smiled, for is he not the god of the children? And the robins among the sparkling frosted holly leaves seemed to chirrup with delight.

And, of course, there were Christmas cards, and one which came from this dear old farmhouse was carefully treasured for many years. It bore a picture of a little girl dressed in a blue frock, a white coat, and ermine muff, and a pale blue hat with a band of fur, a crown of red velvet, and a blue feather. The little fairy was walking down the steps of a house carrying a bunch of holly and mistletoe. After fifty years that card is still remembered, still treasured in memory. Perhaps the dear old hostess, still alive, may have forgotten this card, but the recipient has not.

What a number of things there were to do on this Christmas Day besides stripping the Christmas tree. The blue roan pony, Daniel, had to be visited in his stall, the turkeys and geese inspected, the water wheel visited, and the birds had to have their Christmas dinner. The old squire has passed away, but the old dame still lives, and those children who are left of that merry party still bear in fond remembrance the happy times spent in the old Tudor house. Never a Christmas comes round but the merry scenes are recalled – the happiest Christmas festivals of their lives. It may be today there are far grander presents, far grander parties, but the spirit of hospitality shown by the old folks has never been finer, for they had hearts of gold. How delightful to recall the old days in dear old Somerset, the days of one's childhood, the days when merry Christmas was a real children's festival.

North Curry Reeve's Feast

H.P. OLIVEY

If anywhere in Somerset can claim to have preserved the traditional Christmas it is the village of North Curry, on Sedgemoor between Taunton and Langport. With its neighbours West Hatch and Stoke St Gregory, it has maintained its Christmas 'Reeve's Feast' since the middle ages, and perhaps earlier. Traditionally the feast is associated with King John, who reigned at the beginning of the thirteenth century, although there are theories that it originated in Anglo-Saxon arrangements of land tenure. It is described in detail in a document dated 1314, and was still taking place in much the same way, by immemorial custom, in the early nineteenth century. In 1850, when the custom was in danger of dying out, a local landowner had a tablet inscribed and placed in the church vestry giving full details of the arrangements for the feast. Then in 1868 it was turned into a charity approved by the Charity Commissioners, and in recent years it has been revived. Here is a transcript of the salient details from the tablet in the church.

The Reeve provides the feast and in order to enable him to do so – The lords of the manor allowing the lords rent of the Feast Tenement in respect of which he is appointed to the office, an annual allowance of two pounds by the name of Leaze Fees a

payment of two pounds under the name of Cane Wood and four pounds and five shillings under the name of Beef and Pork.

The Reeve is also allowed by the occupier of the lay rectory 36 bushels of good marketable wheat and 48 shillings in money to be rendered on demand at any time within a month before Christmas annually and likewise by the holders of the undermentioned estates the quantity of wheat set opposite the names of their tenements respectively to be rendered within the like period [Eleven contributors are named, mostly of two bushels each.]

The custom of preparing for and holding the feast is for the Reeve to provide three fat heifers and put them in the manor pound adjoining North Curry churchyard the Sunday before Christmas day, if Christmas happen to be on any other day than Monday or Tuesday, but if it falls on Monday or Tuesday then the Sunday week before Christmas day for the inspection of the persons entitled to the feast, who may insist on having

Postcard greetings from North Curry

them changed if good ones are not provided. Then these are killed by a butcher appointed by the Reeve, and the day before Christmas day delivered with a good half pig to two tenants of the manor of North Curry called dealers, who continue for many years but are annually summoned to their duty by the Reeve and have their vacancies filled up by him.

The dealers are to attend on the day before Christmas day except that day be on a Sunday, and then the day preceding, at the Reeve's with a clerk to cut or deal or dole out the beef and pork to the persons entitled to receive it, and they have provided for them by the Reeve beef stakes [*sic*] and onions for breakfast, top but of beef and three marrow bones boiled with the marrow taken out and spread on toasted bread for dinner, and a feast each of two loaves of bread, eight pennyworth of beef and twopence in money, and one pound of beef suet to be sent home to their houses for their trouble. The dealers serve out two ribs of beef, two ribs of pork, two loaves of bread and twopence in money to each of the holders of the following freehold manors [seven names follow].

They also serve out to the occupiers of two tenements a feast and half, namely three loaves of bread, one shilling's worth of beef and threepence in money. They also serve to the occupiers of the following tenements two loaves of bread, eight pennyworth of beef and twopence in money [140 named tenements follow. Various other measures are allotted to sixteen other tenants.] Each of which loaves of bread is to be made of good white flour. To be well baked and to weigh after baking five pounds, and the beef is to be valued at the price for which beef of the like quality is then currently selling.

To the Reeve of West Hatch within the said manor the dealers serve half a bullock and the hind quarter of half a pig for the use of the tenants of that manor on his paying five shillings for it to the Reeve of North Curry. But before he is allowed to enter the Reeve's house he is to sing the following song:

King John he was a noble knight
I'm come to demand my right
Open the door and let me in
Else I'll carry away my money again.

The dealers serve out these feasts to the persons entitled to them, who are to send for them between sunrise and sunset the day before Christmas day, unless it happen to be on a Sunday, and then the day preceding, and the dealers also serve out for the Reeve a chine, round and rump of beef for mince meat, and the belly part of the fore quarter of the half of pig for a feast to be provided the day after Christmas day except it be a Sunday, and then the day following, by the Reeve for the lords of the manor of Knapp and Slough, who are called the 'Jacks of Knapp and Slough', and have the feast for themselves and their attendants after mentioned. Besides the chief feasts of beef etc in common with the holders of the other five freehold manors they or their deputies arrive at the Reeve's house the feast day about 1 o'clock. The Jack of Knapp or his deputy attended by three men and a boy. And the Jack of Slough or his deputy by two men and a boy.

When the Jack of Knapp or his deputy arrives, the key of the Reeve's cellar (in which there is to be provided a half a hogshead at least of good ale for the feast) is given to one of his attendants. The Jack or deputy proceeds to divide the offal or inferior parts of the bullocks and half pig, not distributed by the dealers to the holders of tenements, into portions to be given away in the afternoon to the second poor. The Jack of Slough or deputy divides six dozen of bread weighing five pounds each loaf when well baked provided by the Reeve for the like purpose.

The Jacks and their attendants then sit down to a dinner provided by the Reeve consisting of the chine of beef roasted and the rump and round boiled, the belly piece of the fore

Thomas atte Sloo, an effigy in North Curry Church. He was one of the lords of Slough manor, commemorated as 'Jack of Slough', who took part in the reeve's feast

quarter of the half pig rolled up and made into a collar of brawn scalded and served up with a sprig of rosemary and powdered with flour, a hen with the head and tail on but the rest of the feathers except the tail plucked off a little boiled and served up on sops of bread, proper vegetables, a large mince pie with an effigy of King John in paste properly painted to represent a king stuck up in the middle of it. Bread and ale and cheese after. When they sit down to dinner two candles weighing a pound each are lighted, and until they are burnt out the Jacks and their attendants have a right to sit drinking ale. After dinner the regular toasts are:

> To the immortal memory of King John.
> The Real Jack of Knapp.
> The Real Jack of Slough.

Afterwards other toasts are given.

The Jacks give away the bread and the offal beef and pork to the second poor. When they have drunk as much as they like, they depart. The Jack of Slough or deputy holding the stirrup of the Jack of Knapp or deputy for him to mount, and receiving a shilling as his fee.

The undersigned declare the above to be the immemorial customs of the feast held annually in the manor of North Curry, and as contributors thereto or partakers thereof they make this recognition for better preserving and keeping up the same [28 signatories].

A Wet Christmas

HENRY HUNT

So a good time was had by all at North Curry. A few miles away, across the Somerset Levels, one man was having a really miserable Christmas. Henry ('Orator') Hunt, the vehement advocate of Parliamentary reform, was sentenced to three years' imprisonment following his speech in Manchester on the occasion of the Peterloo massacre in 1819. Christmas 1821 he spent in Ilchester Gaol (or 'Bastile', as he termed it). Here is part of a letter which he wrote to his supporters on Christmas Eve.

The whole country for miles round Ilchester is under water; and although Mr Fowell Buxton, Mr Baring, Mr Dickenson,

Sir Thomas Lethbridge, and old Sir Isaac Coffin, may say and swear that the Bastile is a dry, healthy, and salubrious Gaol, yet it will not do away with the fact, that it is constantly under water in wet seasons, and that it has been inundated three times within the last six weeks.

A very ludicrous scene took place here yesterday. In the morning the Parson attended to perform divine service in the chapel at the usual time; but before he and Moses, the clerk, had been within the walls ten minutes, the water had risen so rapidly that the prisoners could not pass from their wards to

The Rev.ᵈ T.G.D. THRING,
One of the visiting Magistrates of Ilchester Gaol.
"We must support our own Officers".

Parson Thring of Ilchester, whose discomfiture Henry Hunt describes

the chapel without being half way up to their knees in water. Mr Hardy [the new gaoler] having more regard for the health, comfort and safety of the prisoners than the ex-gaoler, did not choose to compel the poor fellows to sit for two hours with wet feet in a cold chapel, recommended the Parson and Moses to be off as quick as possible, to save themselves from being obliged to swim home out of the Gaol. These worthies readily took the hint to be off, but before they got to the lodge they found that the water had already intercepted their intended flight, it being almost knee-deep in the only road where they could pass. The gaol truck was, in the hurry of the moment, resorted to; and like Neptune and Amphitrite, they mounted this marine car, and hugging each other to avoid being precipitated into the watery element, they were drawn out into the town by four of the prisoners, dressed in zebra coloured jackets, to the great amusement of the multitude who had assembled upon the bridge to witness the novel scene. In the evening my family were happy to embrace the same conveyance.

Mr Thompson, the new surgeon, arrived soon after, not deterred by the flood, although he had ridden his horse nearly a mile through the water, which was up to the skirts of his saddle. When he came here the water was seven inches deep nearly all over the Gaol, and as he could not ride his horse round to the different wards, he mounted upon the back of one of the prisoners, and rode him round; but before he had accomplished his journey, his two-legged horse made a trip, and, falling in the water, unhorsed his rider (whether accidentally or otherwise, is not yet clearly ascertained).

Nothing can exceed the dreadful state of the whole Gaol this day, now the water is sunk, leaving behind a scum and a settlement which emits the most noxious and pestilential exhalations. Three medical men have called upon me this day, to caution me against its deadly effects, and they anticipate, as

Ilchester Bridge and Gaol in 1836, by John Buckler

is usual in this low, flat country, after a flood, that agues and typhus fevers will be very prevalent and fatal. Since my last [letter], new coping stones have been put round the wall of my yard, by the order of Mr Goodford, the Visiting Magistrate. The walls, when the old coping was taken off, were found to be saturated with wet to the very centre; and the new coping does not appear to do the least good this weather. Every well in the Gaol is filled with water out of the drains, and, in fact, all the water that comes into the prison ascends through the drains.

The Turkeys and
the Butcher

*While on the subject of crime and punishment, here is a curious
vignette of country life. You might think that by 27 December
most people have had enough of turkeys – doubly so, in the case
of butchers. But among the Somerset Quarter Sessions Rolls for
1683 there are these three sworn statements made before a
magistrate about an attempted robbery.*

The Informac'on of John Selley of the p'ish of Crocomb in the
County aforesaid [Somerset], Husbandman, taken upon Oath
before me, William Lacy Esqr, one of his Maj'tis Justices of
the Peace for this County the twenty seaventh day of
Decemb'r . . . 1683.

 Saith That being a servant unto Mrs Katherine Carew of
the parish of Crocomb viz. as he was standing in her kitchen
about foure of the clock this morning, John Venn one of his
fellow servants told him there was one w'thout stealing of
Turkeyes. Whereupon this Informant ran' forth and espied
one to whom he sett his dogg who presently ran away and
threw downe a bagg wherein ther was two Turkeyes w'ch he
knew to be his Mistresses, and as the fellow that run' away
from him was goeing over the Mow barton hedge this
Informant caught him by the Legg, his fellow servant John
Ven' coming took off his hatt and then this Informant knew
him to be Jeffry [the rest is missing.]

The Informacon of John Venn of the p'ish of Crocomb in the County aforesaid husbandman taken upon Oath before me William Lacy Esqr . . . the twenty seaventh day of Decemb'r . . . 1683.

Saith That John Selley his fellow servant called him about four of the Clock in the Morning who ariseing heard the Turkeys make a noise, whereupon looking out of the Window he saw some body goe down the Co'rt where the Turkeyes were, then this Informant run out into the Co'rt and seeing somebody goe out at the gate hee went back and called the aforesaid John Selley, who followed and caught him, this Informant coming pr'sently in tooke of his hatt and knew him to be Jeffry Oldman of the p'ish of Crocomb jun'r, butcher, who had dropt a bagg in which was two Turkeyes, the goods of Mrs Katherine Carew of the p'ish of Crocomb aforesaid viz. where upon he hath in suspic'on the said Jeffry Oldman for the stealing of the said Turkeys, and farther saith not. X The mark of John Venn.

The examinac'on of Jeffry Oldman jun'r of the p'ish of Crocomb aforesaid, butcher, had and taken before me William Lacy Esqr . . . the twenty seventh day of Decemb'r . . . 1683.

Saith That about four of the Clock in the Morning he went ov'r the Hedge into Mrs Katherine Carews Backside, but did not take or steale any of her Turkeys w'ch he is accused of by John Selley and John Venn her servants, and farther saith not. Jeffry Oldman.

The sessions rolls do not tell us the magistrate's verdict, but an entry in the relevant order book for a fortnight later reveals that Jeffry Oldman was sentenced to be tied to the back of a moving cart, and whipped.

Lightning Attack

Crowcombe, beneath the Quantocks, was the scene of another dramatic event around Christmas some forty years later, in December 1725. As Henry Hunt has already told us, the weather in Somerset at this time of year can be frightful.

We have the following remarkable account from Crocomb in Somersetshire, viz:– That on Sunday the 20th, between two and three of the clock in the afternoon, whilst the bell was summoning the parishioners to divine service, and not a few of the congregation waited the Revd Minister's coming, some being seated in the church, and others in the church porch;– a very terrible lightning, attended with a most frightful clap of thunder (more loud than a peal of ordnance) attacked the said building. It appeared to the exterior spectators as if a vast number of fire-balls were shot against the steeple; which was shock'd and split in such a strange manner, that the light now penetrates thro' the crevices between the stones in every square or panel. A large stone, of 200lb weight, from between the battlements of the tower and the steeple, was forcibly lifted over the battlements (which are advanced about five feet higher than the place where the said stone was fixed), and thrown into the churchyard. The strong timber which supported the great bell, which was then tolling, was broken in pieces, so that the bell itself fell down; and the window nearest to it was struck quite out, and shattered into innumerable bits, which fell on the ground about twenty yards distant from the tower. The belfry-window, being built of stone, was smitten with such force, that the broken

Crowcombe Church, without its spire, painted by
W.W. Wheatley in 1845. The spire, destroyed by lightning in
1725, reached nearly 25 metres above the tower parapet

splinters flew as thick as hail all about the church and chancel.
The south window of the chancel was also much wrent and
shattered; from which a very ponderous stone falling upon the
communion rail, broke it; and from thence glancing on the
frame of the communion table, destroy'd that in like manner.
The east window of the church was likewise much shock'd and
defac'd, and a hole struck right thro' the wall, three feet thick,
under the same. The outside of the church is much damaged in
various places, and near half of the dial-plate of the clock
broken off. The weather-cock also is much burnt, and in part
broken. Many of the people were struck down; but thro' God's
mercy received no great damage. It was a good providence that
the Minister was not as yet come to the church, or it is very
probable some might have incurred danger, if not loss of life.

A Passing Animal

Floods, thunderbolts . . . whatever next? As New Year's Eve
1893 approached, Somerset was visited by an earthquake. The
Western Gazette *has the details.*

A well-marked shock of earthquake was felt on the northern
side of the Mendip Valley on Saturday night, Dec 30, 1893.
The circumstances seem rather peculiar from the fact that the
shock – or shocks, for it is stated that there were three – were
within a comparatively limited area, and included the towns
of Wells, Shepton Mallet, Glastonbury, and the villages
immediately adjoining these towns. The first shock was felt
about 11.30 pm, accompanied by a rumbling noise, and
lasted for about three seconds. People were awakened out of
their sleep by the rocking of their beds and the clattering of
crockery and falling articles, and some rushed into the streets
in their fright. At 12.28 a second and much more severe
shock was felt, but it was of shorter duration. Both shocks
were felt in all of the towns named and in the surrounding
villages. A third shock about four o'clock is stated to have
been felt by some persons.

In Wells some of the people in St Thomas Street ran out of
their houses, and the residents in Vicars' Close were greatly
alarmed. In some instances crockery ware was thrown from
the dressers and smashed, and at the residence of Mr J.N.
Knight, of Milton, the shock was so great that he thought his
greenhouse boiler had burst, and he got up and examined the
premises. In Shepton Mallet the shock was felt all up one side
of Cowl Street and High Street, and at the district hospital

the beds rocked like hammocks. The shocks were severely felt at Glastonbury and the village of Draycott; whilst at Coxley, people ran out of their houses, others were shaken in their beds, the furniture removed from its place, and in one instance a pillar clock was thrown down and smashed. A second but milder shock occurred at 12.15. The direction appeared to be from south to north. In all the places the effects seem to have been the same, but what was the cause, seeing the limited area? Landslips produce tremors in non-volcanic areas resembling earthquakes, and the falling-in of roofs of subterranean cavities has also been suggested as a cause, but is only likely to affect a small area.

Between 11 and 12 pm on Saturday, two distinct shocks of earthquake were felt in Baltonsborough. The oscillation came northward and travelled one mile southwards. The shocks were preceded by a dull rumbling noise. No damage was done, but fears were entertained for the chimneys, especially on the hill.

An earthquake of considerable violence was experienced in Priddy and the immediate neighbourhood about 11.20 on Saturday night, and another, less violent, about an hour later. The cause of the earthquake would appear to have been a violent subterranean explosion, as the shaking of the earth was accompanied with a dull sound, as of a huge dynamite explosion. The shakings, apparently about six or seven, were quite distinct, lasting about six seconds, and were of such violence as to shake the doors and windows, and in the smelting house of the lead works, shook the dust from the rafters. The second shock lasted only about half the time, and was not nearly so severe. In one house in the parish, through the bolted windows, the ivy was distinctly heard beating against the wall, and rustling as though rubbed violently by a passing animal; this description, that of a

passing animal, is given by others. Another describes it as a huge avalanche of snow slipping from the roof. As far as one could judge, the shock seemed to be travelling in a northerly direction.

A severe shock of earthquake was felt at Wookey on Saturday night, accompanied by a loud rumbling sound. It seemed as if the earth was assuming an undulating motion, such as is observed on the waves of the sea. As nearly as possible it was about 11.20 pm. The animals round were exceedingly restless just then, and the dogs continued to bark for some time afterwards, and were very much disturbed. A second shock was felt at 12.30 on Sunday morning. This was quite different, and seemed more of a tremor than the other, causing things to rattle, pictures to sway, and windows to shake. A third shock was noticed by some about four o'clock, but it was very slight.

At Wookey Hole the shocks of earthquake were very severe under the hills. The first was preceded by what seemed a terrific explosion; persons were thrown from the chairs and from bed. The first shock occurred on the 30th at 11.20 pm; the second shock at 12.28 was not accompanied by so much noise, but was much more violent, for the houses and everything on the shelves vibrated about two seconds.

The Snow Dumpling

RICHARD WALTER

We do not expect earthquakes at Christmas. What we do expect, and some of us hope for, is snow. And we are always ready to accept that winters were harder long ago, with mountains of snow and months of permafrost. A note in a copy of a history of Glastonbury, now in the Somerset Record Office, would have us believe the following:

In this Emperour's (Claudius Drusius emperor of the Romans) reign there was so hard a frost that all the lakes and rivers were passable from the middle of November to the beginning of April. A cow at Glasenbury brought forth a lamb. And a star appeared triangular darting its fiery beams like swords and javelins towards the Earth for three weeks.

Be that as it may, heavy snowfall could certainly have unforeseen consequences.

The following ballad, written by Richard Walter in the middle of the last century, was taken from his manuscript notes and communicated to the *Somerset County Herald* by Dr R. Hensleigh Walter, who adds that the song used to be sung at the Club festival of the Prince of Wales Friendly Society at the inn on the top of Ham Hill.

Exmoor in winter's icy grip

By the roadside between Stoke and Cartgate, adjoining the lane leading to Rixon, there formerly (1830) stood a thatched cottage, in which lived Jack Hayne, a pensioner [i.e. a former serviceman], commonly known as 'Captain' Hayne, and his wife Betty, who lived a cat-and-dog life. Betty used occasionally to go to Yeovil shopping, and on one occasion during a snowstorm was benighted on her way home over Ham Hill and was lost until morning. This inspired the following verses:

I'll sing ye a song, 'tis a rather rum joke,
About an old 'ooman that lived up to Stoke,
Who went into Yeovil for 'baccy to smoke,
And some snuff and some tea which she put in her poke.
(Refrain): Ri-too-ral-loo-ral-loo-ral-lay,
        Ri-too-ral-loo-ral-lay.

A Somerset Christmas

The wind did blow and the snow came down,
'Twas as dark as pitch afore she left town;
She took but a drop o' good gin at the Crown,
And away she toddled o'er Odcombe Down.
      Ri-too-ral, etc.

It was such a night as one seldom sees,
The snow was deep, and hard it did freeze;
So she lighted her pipe to keep out the breeze,
But at every step she was up to her knees.
      Ri-too-ral, etc.

She lost her way, but she struggled on till
She got to the top of Hamdon Hill,
When she made a slip, and against her will
Down she rolled like a rat in a mill.
      Ri-too-ral, etc.

The snow gathered round her and formed a ball,
As round as a dumpling but not so small.
It rolled and rolled until the wall
At the bottom received it and stopped its fall.
      Ri-too-ral, etc.

When Betty had finished her comical roll,
She thought that her quarters were rather droll;
So she up wi' her stick and she poked a hole
To let out the 'baccy smoke – cunning wold soul!
      Ri-too-ral, etc.

She thought it a long and a terrible night,
For her nose and her knees were doubled up tight;
But still she kept puffing wi' all her might,
And wondered how long afore 'twould be light.
      Ri-too-ral, etc.

Next morning Jack Hayne came whistling wi' glee;
He was 'mazed such a smoke from a snowball to see;
He gave it a kick – Lor' how stared he!
When out bundled Betty as brisk as a bee.
  Ri-too-ral, etc.

The Old Man's Christmas Story

G.F. MUNFORD

The misfortune of becoming lost in the snow is the subject of our next piece, a Christmas ghost story told with a beautifully judged sense of melodrama. It was written by G.F. Munford for his collection of Ghosts and Legends of South Somerset, *published in 1922.*

Aye! draw around the fire, and I will tell the tale once more. I always think of it at Christmas time, and at the very sight of a snowflake that night's adventure rushes into my memory and makes me shudder.

I forget the year now, but it was during that memorable winter when there were twenty feet of snow upon the ground – when the tops of the trees were the only traces of vegetation – when the hedges were totally covered with the purest of

white mantles, and no guide was left for the traveller but his own untutored instinct.

There never could be a brighter moonlight night, and when I set out on my journey from Chard to Crewkerne – about ten o'clock – the moon, which was nearly full, shone with such lustre upon the snow that the pure soft silvery light flung a kind of enchanted halo over the earth. If only for the scenery, my memory of that night will never fade.

Fear! I knew not what it meant, and cared but little for the ghosts and hobgoblins which are known to haunt that road – for, to tell the truth, I did not then believe in them. I was well wrapped up, and, with a stout stick as my only companion, I started with a light heart across the unbeaten desert of snow which lay before me – walking as straight as I could in the direction in which I knew Crewkerne lay.

For the first three or four miles I was confident of my own sagacity, but, after walking about an hour and a half – having seen no trace of a house, not even Windwhistle Inn, which I fully expected to pass – I began to fancy that I had taken the wrong course. I was getting terribly tired – for it was hard work to wade through the snow – and my heart began to beat fast as I thought of the probability of being lost and of the horror of death from cold and hunger. All the courage I had at starting evaporated – I was fairly unmanned – and I stood still in that bleak snowy desert, not knowing which way to steer, and almost cried. I thought of my home and of the comforts which I knew awaited me there, and cursed my foolhardiness for venturing across the pathless waste. The owls, who could find no resting-place except on the tops of the tallest trees, were loud in their midnight revels, and kept up a continual 'Ch'wit! ch'woo!' as if in mockery of my perplexity.

Whilst my thoughts were racked with the dilemma, and I was considering whether I should turn to the right or left, or whether I should keep in the way I was going, or re-trace my

steps, I saw, far off in the pale moonlight, what appeared to be the chimney of a cottage, and hastily made my way thither, with the view of ascertaining the direction I ought to take for Crewkerne. It was a cottage, and what was more, it was inhabited. But it was literally snowed in, and the only means of going in or coming out of the house was through the bedroom window, and at that I rattled violently to arouse the occupants of the room.

It was some time before I received my answer, although I plainly heard the rough voice of a man, the tremulous notes of a woman, and the plaintive whispers of several children – all of whom were evidently in a state of great alarm. Thinking that my intrusion had been the cause thereof, I shouted, asking for two or three hours shelter, and telling them that I had lost my way.

The rough voice was in favour of admitting me, but I heard the woman say, in an earnest tone: 'For God's sake, Robert, don't think of such a thing! It's that dreadful smuggler's ghost again! Oh, we will leave this terrible place!' And then she burst out crying.

'Nonsense!' replied her stern companion. 'Ghosts can't talk! 'Tis a poor traveller who has lost his way. Let's pull up the curtain and open the window. If it's anybody who means any harm he shall soon feel the contents of this pistol!'

He was, I suppose, about to open the window, but the entreaties of his wife, and the screams of his children – all of whom declared that it was the 'smuggler's ghost' – prevented him from doing so.

'If you won't give me shelter,' I said, 'will you do me the favour to tell me the direction I must take for Crewkerne.'

'Keep a little to your left, and follow straight on,' replied Robert. 'You will then come to Coombe Farm, when you'll know where you are.'

'Yes, if ever I get there. But where am I now?'

'Fox in Snow', from *Wild Exmoor through the Year* by E.W. Hendy

'At Purtington. Keep to your left and you'll make no mistake. Good-night.'

'Good-night,' I growled, surlily enough, you may depend upon it – for I thought them unnaturally inhospitable.

I followed in the direction I was told without the slightest hope of ever finding my way, and wondering deeply what on earth the people could have meant by their strange behaviour and by their allusion to the 'Smuggler's Ghost'. 'Ch'wit! Ch'woo!' rejoiced the owls, as I again plodded mechanically on. My limbs were stiff with cold, and I felt dreadfully afraid that I should fall across the ghost to which those nervous people had alluded. Snow, snow, everywhere – except up there, where the moon and stars looked down upon me in silent majesty! So overwhelming was the scene that I believe I should have swooned and dreamed of being in fairy-land but for the hideous screaming of the owls.

In the midst of the dismal chorus, a fearful heart-rending

scream burst upon my ears – a long agonizing shriek – too wild for human utterance. It began in the distance, travelled with the chilly night-air across my path, hung among the far-off hills, came back again and again, and ultimately died into a groaning wail!

Whilst I stood paralysed with fear, a riderless horse, saddled and bridled, plunged out from among the tops of the trees of Blackmoor Copse, on my right, and dashed at full speed towards the spot on which I was rivetted. Another horse, but with a rider on its back urging it at full speed, came close behind. And yet a third, also with a rider, plunging recklessly after the second! I was not alone then, but I prayed for my solitariness to return.

Oh, 'tis too, too horrible to tell! The first horse – as if mad with fright – ran close to me, snorted a deathly dampness, and dashed on, and on, and on! I saw it no more.

The second horse was ridden by a grim surly-looking fellow, with a pistol in his belt and a dagger by his side. He had on a slouched hat, and pulled it over his eyes as if to hide his face. But the diabolical leer in his countenance could not be hidden with a thousand coverings! Oh, how he urged his horse and kept looking behind him as if fearful that his pursuer would overtake him! And what a sense of strangling suffocation was flung over me as the fiendish form glided close to my side! I could not move – try how I would.

The third whirled past me with the same haste, and he, I saw, was dressed in the uniform of a coastguard. His hand eagerly grasped a pistol, and his face bore a wild and excited look I shall never forget, but not half so fiendish as the other.

The first horse took a circular direction, as if uncertain which way to go. On and on they plunged. The pace increased. And they were both coming towards me again! I fell upon my knees – I could not help it – and the owls laughed with joy. A strange thing was that the horses made

no noise. The trampling of the animals could not be expected to sound amongst the soft snow, but there was no jingling of rein or stirrup, and neither rider uttered a word. Yet their looks betrayed a fearful meaning.

On and on! The pursued horseman urged his steed at the rate of an express train, and was bearing towards me at a frightful pace. But his pursuer gradually gained, and just as the grim-looking rider came close to me – crouched trembling amongst the snow – the pistol of the coastguard flashed its fatal messenger and put for ever a stop to the speed of the horse he was pursuing.

In an instant – in the twinkling of an eye – the rider leaped upon his feet, drew his pistol, and shot the horse of the coastguardsman dead! Another mysterious thing was that the pistols made no reports. But the long forked tongues of fire were plain enough, God knows!

I thought it must be a horrible dream, and mechanically moved my arms as if to wrap myself in the bedclothes. There was another moment's lull, in which both riders confronted each other with savage looks, each holding a dagger in his hand in readiness to strike a blow. Oh! What a deathly atmosphere surrounded me! All my imaginary bedclothes failed to keep it off. And the moon shone on those lifeless horses, and on those diabolical human forms – but no shadow was cast, no noise was heard – except the dismal chanting of the owls.

'Am I going mad?' I thought, 'or is it a frightful nightmare?' For I could not rise from my crouching position, although I saw those two men within a few yards of me engaged in a deadly struggle!

They closed. The one with the slouched hat then got the better of his antagonist, and, with a horrible leer of fiendish triumph, struck the dagger violently into his bosom!

There was another wild agonizing cry, which echoed and

re-echoed along the snowy expanse, and which must have startled every living thing for miles – the owls again laughing their unearthly laugh of exultation!

The murderer wiped his dagger upon the ground – leaving a long red track – and hurriedly glided away, taking no notice of me, the unwilling witness of the foul deed.

All was done in much less time than I can tell it. But it seemed an age to me, and I was so petrified with fear that I thought I should have turned into a stone. After the murderer had departed, I felt much relieved, and the power of which I seemed deprived returned.

So I rose to my feet and went to the murdered man, thinking that I should perhaps be of some service to him. But, from what I have since heard, I was nearly fifty years too late!

I stopped and endeavoured to take hold of the arm that was stretched out upon the snow. But, good God! I found that I grasped at nothing! There was the form – stark and motionless – the rigid features in the horrible contortion, as if writhing in agony! – there was that blood oozing out of the wound and making a dark trail along the pure white snow! – and there were the two horses lying lifeless at his feet! I then became aware that what I had seen was only a phantom tragedy!

'Ch'wit! Ch'woo!' laughed the owls again. And the keen frosty air became full of such fiendish yells as pierced my very soul. All around me, and in the distance, there were such loud and discordant noises as if the orchestra of Hell had been let loose! I could endure the scene no longer – my nerves were completely unstrung – and I swooned by the side of those livid phantom corpses! – on a desert of snow, and with an uninterrupted chorus of owl-music as a dismal lullaby.

It must have been some time before I rallied, for when I awoke the day was beginning to break, and I was so

benumbed and stupefied with cold that I hardly had the power to move. My brain was in a whirl. I looked around, but could see no evidence of a struggle. No corpses were there then, and no tracks upon the snow were discernible except those I had made myself! I then found that I was in Coombe Farm Valley, and I made my way home as fast as the weakened state I was in would allow me.

The story is not quite finished. I naturally fell ill and was seized with a fever brought on by the exposure and fright, and was ill for many weeks. When I first told my adventure, it was thought to be the invention of a disordered brain. But as soon as I was well enough – by which time the snow had disappeared – I found out the people who lived at the cottage to which I had applied for shelter.

Robert remembered my calling perfectly well, and told me that not long afterwards, on that very night, three horsemen passed his cottage in full chase.

'They were the ghosts of three men who often ride by this way in the middle of wintry nights,' said he. 'The first always stops opposite my house and hastily motions as if to ask for shelter. Immediately afterwards, the two others come on at full gallop, and all three bound off across the country. They do say that they are the ghosts of two coastguardsmen and a smuggler who murdered them about fifty or sixty years ago. But about that I know nothing. All I know is that they often chase each other across the valley. And the reason I did not let you in was because my wife and children were afraid that you were the ghost of the smuggler seeking for shelter.'

I told him what I had seen, and he assured me that the tragedy had often been witnessed exactly as I have described it.

A Black Day

ELIZABETH GOUDGE

Not all Christmas dramas are quite so calamitous and bloodcurdling. Most disappointments and unhappinesses are on a smaller scale, although in the mind of a child minor setbacks can take on epic proportions. Elizabeth Goudge wrote her novel about Wells, A City of Bells, *in 1936, although it is set during the First World War. The grandfather of the story is a canon of Wells Cathedral, and the following episode takes place on 29 December.*

The day after the party was the day chosen by Grandfather for the children's annual lesson on the connection between Faith and Works, and it was a black day. Faith, as understood by Henrietta and Hugh Anthony, was saying your prayers and going to church and this they had no objection to, but Works was giving away your toys to the poor and that was another thing altogether. What connection was there, they demanded indignantly of each other, between kneeling in your nightgown at the side of your bed at night and saying 'Our-Father-witchard-in-heaven,' followed by 'Now-I-lay-me,' and parting next day from the doll's perambulator and the tin helmet?. . . There seemed none.

The giving away of the toys always took place in the afternoon, and in the morning, as soon as breakfast was over, Grandfather and the children withdrew to the little room half-way up the tower where the toy-cupboards were kept. They toiled up the stone stairs, carrying two large baskets and

the oil-stove that was to warm them during their melancholy employment, in a depressing silence.

The little room had been given to the children because it was like a room in a fairy tale. It was nearly at the top of the tower and its mullioned window, set in the thickness of the wall, had a lovely view of the Cathedral towers, the Tor and the jumbled roofs of the city. It was quite empty, except for the children's treasures, and in it they were never required to tidy up.

They had a cupboard each whose state, Grandfather thought, was typical of their owners. In Henrietta's cupboard her dolls, together with their garments, furniture, crockery and cooking utensils, were laid out in neat rows on the top shelf. Her books were on the second shelf and treasures such as ribbons, tinsel off the Christmas-tree and boxes of beads were on the third shelf. You could see at once where everything was, and what it was, and when you opened the cupboard door nothing fell out. With Hugh Anthony's cupboard it was not so, for as soon as the door was opened an avalanche descended. Jumbled up among engines with their wheels off, cricket bats cracked in the middle, headless soldiers and a moth-eaten golliwog who had seen better days, were chestnuts, bits of silver-paper, birds' feathers, the skin of a defunct snake, a mangel-wurzel and, most horrible of all, a baby chicken with two heads which had been preserved in a bottle of spirits and given to Hugh Anthony by Bates two Christmases ago. . . Hugh Anthony with his scientific mind adored this chicken and could never understand why everyone else averted their eyes when it was produced.

Having lit the oil-stove Grandfather sat himself down on the old rocking-horse and proceeded to superintend. Each child was required to fill a basket, but they were not required to give away anything they had received this Christmas. They chose themselves what they should give away and Grandfather only interfered when he considered the choice unsuitable.

The cupboards were opened, the avalanche fell and work began.

Hugh Anthony always started by picking out the things that he really did not want, the heads of the soldiers, for instance, and the moth-eaten golliwog, but Grandfather's voice would thunder out behind him, 'No, Hugh Anthony! Rubbish must not be given to God's poor!' Then Hugh Anthony, after getting no answer to his 'Why not?' which Grandfather considered a rhetorical question unworthy of answer, would be obliged to choose instead the soldiers that were very nearly intact and the least beloved of his engines, pistols and bricks. The things that he cared for most deeply, such as the two-headed chicken and the skin of the snake, Grandfather mercifully considered unsuitable.

Henrietta was the stuff of which martyrs are made, for when she had to give away she always gave what she loved best. Grandfather, as he watched her dark head bent sadly over the basket and her dainty fingers slowly placing her treasures side by side inside it, understood her and suffered agonies. Yet he never interfered with the suggestion that Gladys Hildegarde, the least-loved of Henrietta's dolls, would do just as well to give away as Irene Emily Jane the worshipped and adored. . . No. . . For who knew what spiritual strength and beauty might not pass from Henrietta to the sawdust bosom of Irene Emily Jane, and from thence to the little girl to whom she would be given?

But the sacrifice of this lady had taken place a year ago and she was now forgotten, for time heals even the worst of wounds. Henrietta had this year, so her conscience said, to part from the snowstorm that Miss Lavender had given her on her birthday. It was an incomparable toy. It consisted of a glass globe inside which a red man in a yellow hat stood on a green field. His cottage stood in the middle distance while to the right was a fir-tree and to the left a dog. This in itself was amazing, for how in the world did the red man, his cottage,

his dog and the fir-tree get inside the globe? But there was a greater marvel yet to come, for when the globe was held upside down it began to snow. First a few flakes fell, then a few more, then they fell so thick and fast that the man and his house and his dog and the fir-tree were hidden from sight. Then you turned the globe right way up again and the storm ceased. . . It was amazing. . . Henrietta took it out of the cupboard and held it in her hands, her head bent. Then for the last time she held it upside down and watched the snow fall. Then she placed it in the basket and turned her back on it.

Grandfather watched her with painful attention and her action seemed to him to take on a mystic meaning. The globe was the world itself, containing all creation, trees, animals, man and his works, the earth and the sky, and Henrietta, it seemed, was one of those rare beings who are prepared for love's sake to see 'the universe turn to a mighty stranger'.

After she had parted with the snowstorm it seemed to Henrietta quite easy to part with other things; with her necklace of blue beads, her set of drawing-room furniture made by herself out of chestnuts, with pins for legs and pink wool twisted round more pins for the back of the chairs, her toy sewing-machine and her Dolly Dimple, a cardboard person with twelve sets of cardboard underclothes, and ten hats.

When the baskets were packed they went downstairs and Grandfather read to them to cheer them up, and after that there was a rather penitential dinner of boiled cod and rice pudding at which Hugh Anthony did not behave well.

'Will you have skin, Hugh Anthony?' asked Grandmother, for she did not make the children eat milk-pudding-skin if they did not want to.

'No,' said Hugh Anthony shortly.

'No, what?' asked Grandmother, who was punctilious about 'thank you' being inserted in the proper place.

'No skin,' said Hugh Anthony.

The Missletoe Bough

THOMAS HAYNES BAYLY

Here is another Christmas tragedy, possibly with a basis in fact. 'The Missletoe Bough' is a sentimental ballad which enjoyed great popularity among the Victorians. Its author was a native of Bath, who died in 1839, and it was set to music by Henry Bishop, better known as the composer of 'Home, Sweet Home'. Several places have been suggested as the inspiration for the story, including Marwell Hall, near Winchester. But Somerset historians claim that the source is Bawdrip, near Bridgwater, and it is certainly true that the church boasts a monument (inconveniently hidden behind the altar) which tells of Eleanor Lovel. She died in 1681, 'snatched away on her wedding day by a sudden and untimely fate. . .' This, according to the ballad, is what happened to her.

The missletoe hung in the castle hall,
The holly branch shone on the old oak wall
And the baron's retainers were blithe and gay
And keeping their Christmas holiday
The baron beheld with a father's pride
His beautiful child, young Lovell's bride,
While she with her bright eyes seemed to be
The star of that goodly company.
Oh the missletoe bough, oh the missletoe bough.

I'm weary of dancing now she cried
Here tarry a moment, I'll hide, I'll hide,
And Lovell be sure thou'st the first to trace
The clue to my secret lurking place
Away she ran, and her friends began
Each tower to search, and each nook to scan
And Lovell cried Oh, where dost thou hide
I'm lonesome without thee, my own dear bride.
Oh the missletoe bough, Oh the missletoe bough.

They sought her that night, and they sought her next day
And they sought her in vain when a week passed away
In the highest, the lowest, the loneliest spot
Young Lovell sought wildly, but found her not
And years flew by, and their grief at last
Was told as a sorrowful tale long past
And when Lovell appeared, the children cried
See the old man weeps for his fairy bride.
Oh the missletoe bough, Oh the missletoe bough.

At length an oak chest that had long lain hid
Was found in the castle, they raised the lid
And a skeleton form lay mouldering there
In the bridal wreath of the lady fair
Oh sad was her fate. In sportive jest
She hid from her lord in the old oak chest
It closed with a spring, and her bridal bloom
Lay withering there in a living tomb.
Oh the missletoe bough, Oh the missletoe bough.

Burnham-on-Santa

The following mishap had less tragic consequences. This account was published by the Burnham-on-Sea Gazette *in December 1945.*

ALARMING INCIDENT AT BAZAAR
'Father Christmas' Lit a Cigarette

An alarming incident occurred at the bazaar in the Burnham-on-Sea Town Hall on Saturday. When 'Father Christmas' impersonated by Mr Percy Sealey, of 29 Abingdon Street, was lighting a cigarette, his whiskers caught fire. The hall was crowded and grown-up people nearby with great promptitude threw clothing over him, and the flames were quickly extinguished.

'Father Christmas' was rushed to the Burnham-on-Sea Hospital, but happily not detained and he was able to return home comparatively little the worse for his experience. He received slight burns about the back of the neck and left hand, and shock. He attended at the hospital on subsequent days of the week to have the injuries dressed.

The Waning of Bethlehem's Star

Next we turn to another of the great institutions of Christmas, the Nativity Play – and, once again, things do not turn out quite as expected.

Three days after Christmas in 1915, at the Crispin Hall in Street, the first performance took place of a musical nativity

A nativity play, staged by unemployed members of Bath Good Neighbours Club in 1935

play, which was subsequently published, adopted by amateur choral societies, and performed around the world. Its title was *Bethlehem*, and it was the work of a composer now for the most part forgotten, but famous for a few years in the 1920s. His name was Rutland Boughton.

Bethlehem is very decidedly a Somerset nativity play. The three shepherds, whose names are Jem, Dave and Sym, have broad West-Country accents, and, when the first of the wise men enters, his song is derived from a Somerset folk tune. The keynote to the drama's success is its simplicity. It is based on the well-known Coventry mystery plays, with Arthurian overtones, and includes several popular carols which, at the original performances, the audience were encouraged to join the performers in singing. The score is tuneful, and much of it sounds like folksong (although only the one genuine folk melody is used); it is not too difficult for amateurs to sing,

Rutland Boughton on his smallholding in Gloucestershire, after the failure of the Glastonbury Festival movement

and there are plenty of homely touches — the gifts which the shepherds bring for the infant Jesus are a whistle, a hat and a pair of mittens. Contemporary events are alluded to, for example when Herod describes himself as 'the mightiest lord and Kaiser that ever walked on ground'.

To explain the significance of the play's links with Somerset, including its first performance here, we have to go back a year, to 1914, and the first of the Glastonbury Festivals. Rutland Boughton was an idealist, whose dream during the years before the war had been to establish a native British opera (he preferred the description 'music drama') based on Celtic and Arthurian legends, just as Wagner had used Teutonic legends to create German opera. Part of the plan was to find an appropriate venue where the works could be performed, and where a kind of 'co-operative' of artists and musicians could live together to experiment and create. Nowadays the term to describe such an endeavour would be a 'workshop'. Surrey woodland near Hindhead was considered, and Letchworth Garden City, but in 1913 Glastonbury was agreed upon, and after a few setbacks (including the declaration of war the same day) the first Glastonbury Festival began on 5th August 1914 — and the Assembly Rooms, down an alleyway behind the High Street, became England's answer to Wagner's Bayreuth.

Supported by the Clark family of Street and other well-wishers, including George Bernard Shaw, the festival overcame its difficulties, and Boughton's dream became a reality. By 1922 he could boast that the Glastonbury Festival Movement had to date staged 266 performances of operas, plays and ballets, 54 concerts and over 500 classes in singing, dancing and similar subjects. What is more, one of the music dramas, *The Immortal Hour*, in that year transferred to the London stage, where it was to achieve a run of 216 consecutive performances — a world record for serious opera that has never been broken. Rutland Boughton became the toast of the musical establishment.

It was a bewildering and unsettling time for the composer. A man of strong socialist and musical principles, he felt uncomfortable in the West End. Matters came to a head in 1926. For the Christmas season he staged a revival of *Bethlehem*, but because of his disgust at the General Strike, and the treatment meted out to the miners, he decided (without consulting his Glastonbury colleagues) to dispense with the traditional trappings of the nativity play, and to set the drama in a miner's cottage, with the characters in modern dress. Herod became a decadent capitalist, and his courtiers included policemen and soldiers.

The religious establishment of the day, which understandably felt a certain possessiveness about the nativity and the way in which it was portrayed, voiced its objections, Boughton fell out with his fellow directors, the production made a loss, and the whole enterprise was effectively bankrupted. The local Glastonbury newspaper, the *Central*

Rutland Boughton's autograph, with four bars from his most celebrated work, *The Immortal Hour*

Somerset Gazette, announced the following July that the festival would not be held that year. An emergency meeting of the festival company had been held, and had decided to go into voluntary liquidation. Mr Boughton, the principal creditor (he was owed £400), told the newspaper that he would carry on the work of producing English operas himself.

And so the celebrated composer found that his career had gone from rags to riches to rags again, and he retired to a smallholding near Newent in Gloucestershire, from where, indeed, he did make occasional attempts to restart his English opera festival movement. He died in 1960 and, apart from one song from *The Immortal Hour*, his life and work have been largely forgotten. Until now, that is, for perhaps now the tide is turning. There are commercial recordings available of both *Bethlehem* and *The Immortal Hour*, and one hopes that, as the qualities of Boughton's music become appreciated again, before long Somerset people will again be able to enjoy live performances of their own nativity play.

The Dark Visitor

W.G. WILLIS WATSON

After Rutland Boughton's world of mingled pagan, Christian and secular traditions, it seems appropriate to record a selection of the Christmas and New Year sayings which were still to be heard in Somerset when he was writing his dramas. These were

A Somerset Christmas

*collected by Willis Watson for his newspaper column in 1919,
and they take us through the festive season from Christmas Eve
to Twelfth Night.*

Christmas Eve

It is said that ghosts never appear on Christmas Eve.

It is considered unlucky to start decorating the house before Christmas Eve.

If a maiden sleeps on Christmas Eve on a bed unadorned with a holly spray, she is quite certain to be visited with all manner of evil spirits and goblins to punish her for her omission of the time-honoured sacred rite.

Christmas Day

If it snows during Christmas night the crops will do well.

If at Christmas ice hangs on the willow, clover may be cut at Easter.

If ice will bear a man at Christmas it will not bear a mouse afterwards.

A light Christmas a heavy sheaf.

A mild Christmas makes work for the Sexton.

If the sun shines through the apple trees on Christmas day an abundant crop of apples may be expected in the following year.

At Christmas a capon, at Michaelmas a goose. And somewhat else at New Year's Tide for fear the lease flies loose.

If Christmas Day on a Sunday fall, a troublous winter we shall have all.

Boxing Day (St Stephen's Day)

If you bleed your nag on St Stephen's Day,
He'll work your work for ever and aye.

St John's Day (27th December)
Yule is come and Yule is gone,
And we have feasted well
So Jack must to his flail again,
And Jenny to her wheel.

New Year's Eve
The year does nothing else but open and shut.
Say no ill of the year till it be past.
If New Year's Eve night the wind blow south,
  It betokeneth warmth and growth;
If west much milk and fish in the sea;
  If north much cold and storms there will be;
If east the trees will bear much fruit;
  If north-east flee it man and brute.

New Year's Day
Trimming the nails is as much to be avoided on New Year's day as it is of a Sunday, of which the rhyme is often quoted: 'Cut 'em on Sunday, you cut 'em for evil, for the rest of the week you'll be ruled by the Devil.' Substitute 'New Year' and 'year' where required, and you have the ban on the operation.

The first person that crosses the threshold to enter the house on New Year's day, if he be a dark man, brings luck. The darker the first visitor is the more luck he brings. A sandy or red-haired man will bring evil days to the house.

It is lucky to give away money and food on New Year's day.

The child who is born on New Year's day will bring good luck to all the family.

The housewife who sweeps her house before the sun has shone on New Year's morn will be unfortunate.

To obtain good fortune you must go out for the first time on New Year's day empty-handed and come in full; thus you will receive more than you give away during the year.

If a robin fly against the window during New Year's day it is a sign that someone in the house will die before the year is out.

Tie the garter of the left leg in two bows below the knee on New Year's day to prevent being bewitched during the year.

Old Christmas Eve (5th January)

Never pick Holy Thorn on Old Christmas eve when you hear the cracking of the buds, or you will receive a curse.

As the clock strikes midnight the finest and handsomest beast of the herd, called 'the master bullock', lows softly and musically three times, and then goes down on his knees before the manger. Every west-country farmer believes this as fully as he does in the existence of Dunkery Beacon.

Old Christmas Day or Epiphany (6th January)

It was formerly believed that if Old Christmas day came during a waxing moon a good year would follow; if during the waning moon it prognosticated a hard year, and the nearer the end of the moon the worse were the expectations.

If the sun shines before noon on Old Christmas day there will be an abundance of apple blossom and fruit during the year. Also if the sun shines through the apple trees on that day it will be a good cider year.

On Old Christmas day no horse owner will allow a horse to be taken for use out of his stables. Anyone who rides or drives on that day is certain to meet with an accident, as it is believed that this day is the horse's special holiday.

At Epiphany the ploughmen take their Twelfth cake and Wassail bowl into the ox-house and wassail the stock.

Washerwomen refuse to wash on this day – 'It's unlucky; it's throwing soapsuds in the Saviour's face.'

Oh, No, It Isn't!

THOMAS FORDER PLOWMAN

One more Christmas tradition, so far overlooked in this collection, is the pantomime. The first Bath pantomime seems to have taken place on Boxing Day 1850, and was advertised thus:

THEATRE ROYAL, BATH
under the management of Mrs Macready.
The Nobility, Gentry, and Public are respectfully informed that the theatre will open on Thursday Dec 26 1850 with a new comic grand CHRISTMAS PANTOMIME, being a new version of the History of England – Romantically, though Historically, rendered – Local, yet Legendary – called HARLEQUIN TEMPLAR; or, Richard Couer de Lion taking in Bath on his way to Palestine; an Incident not to be found in either Hume, Smollett, Goldsmith, or Macaulay.

The Opening and Comic Scenes written and invented expressly for this Theatre; the Overture and Music composed, arranged, and selected by Mr. Salmon; the Scenery, entirely new, designed and executed by Mr. F. Thorne, Mr. Stanley, and Assistants. The Properties, Masks, and Paraphernalia, by Messrs Howey, Lodge, and Ashwell; the extensive Machinery, Tricks, and Transformations, by Messrs Horwell and Wiltshire; the Dresses, by Miss Quick and Assistants.

The HARLEQUINADE will be supplied by Metropolitan Performers of the First Celebrity. Clown: Mr. Grammani. Harlequin: Mr. Osmond. Pantaloon: Herr Karl. Columbine: Mlle. Rosina.

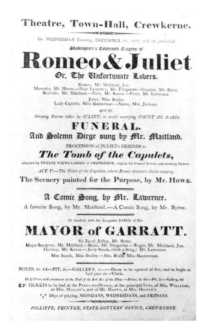

A strange mixture for theatre-goers at Crewkerne, on Christmas Eve, 1817

Thursday Dec 26, and following evenings. Previous to the Pantomime, the Comic Piece of 'THE INNKEEPER'S WIFE'. Characters by the Company. To conclude with the Farce of 'The Two Gregories'.

This was how it was noticed by the Bath Chronicle *the following week:*

The new Christmas pantomime was produced on the evening of Thursday last. Its title is 'Harlequin Templar; or Richard Couer de Lion taking in Bath on his way to the Holy Land'. The piece has been got up with great care and

considerable cost; and its success has been complete. The introductory *libretto* is extremely comic, and it has been received with shouts of the heartiest laughter. As may be inferred from the title of the pantomime, there are numerous local allusions. These have been conceived in a spirit of capital humour, and are such as cannot give offence in any quarter. The scenery is very good – the dresses and disguises are capital – the fun never flags – and the tricks and transformations very cleverly executed. The music consists of adaptations of very pleasing popular airs; and this department of the entertainment is alone amply worth a visit to the Theatre. The various characters are supported with great vivacity. Each scene has its particular claim to approbation; but we may single out for especial notice the fight between the 'armies' of Richard and Saladin, than which we never witnessed anything more irresistibly ludicrous. It has nightly thrown the house into uncontrollable fits of laughter. We heartily recommend those of our playgoing readers who may not have seen the Pantomime not to lose the opportunity of doing so. They will have an abundant return of rich amusement for their money.

The Bath pantomime became an institution, to such an extent that even someone who went on to be one of the city's mayors tried his hand at it in the 1890s. He was Thomas Forder Plowman, mayor in 1912, and in his autobiography he candidly mused on his shortcomings.

My theatrical experiences would hardly be complete if I did not confess that once upon a time I had the hardihood to attempt the regeneration of pantomime, and there were people good enough to think that I did accomplish something in that direction, but, if so, the effect was very transient. I must admit that, viewed from an author's standpoint, the result fell far short of my hopes and aspirations. In my

Crewkerne's Boxing-Day
entertainment in 1817 promised
to end with a miller and his mill
being blown to atoms

simplicity I fancied that both the public and the profession
might take kindly to a stage-version of a pretty fairy story, so
presented that the main incidents, accepted and believed in
from time immemorial, followed in proper sequence without
incoherent interruptions, thus sustaining the interest in the
plot to the finish. I thought, too, that the traditional old
woman – a man in petticoats – with an acknowledged craving
for alcoholic drinks, and a flightiness of disposition out of
harmony with her years, might be made more sober and
respectable. I likewise believed that the red-nosed
'knockabouts', who were wont to burst upon the scene clad in
modern garments of a flamboyant type, might be dispensed

with. I sought also to disestablish other freakish monstrosities, which I need not specify. Then it was part of my scheme that every rhyming couplet should have its proper number of feet, neither more nor less; that its scansion should pass muster; that the rules of rhyme should be strictly observed; and that the whole should go trippingly on the tongue. Of course, the popular songs of the day had to be utilised, but I adapted the words to the particular situation they were intended to illustrate.

Alas, I lost sight of the fact that the average pantomime company, wedded to ancient traditions, regarded what I looked upon as mere excrescences as absolute essentials, whilst the ordinary stage-manager cared for none of the things that I thought all-important! So my efforts to substitute something in the way of humour more subtle than horseplay and a mere kicking up behind and before, and to introduce a touch of sentiment here and there, often had to give way to interpellations [*sic*] that made me shudder and played havoc with my fairy-story. In a sylvan glade in Fairyland, a comedian, who had previously got into a brilliant check suit specially for the purpose, would suddenly burst upon the scene in order to impress upon the audience in song that 'At Trinity Church I met my doom', or to vocalise something akin to it, equally foreign to the situation. I would say to him, 'But, my dear sir, if you *must* sing that song, I will write words for it that shall be more in harmony with the spirit of the scene, and you can sing it in a garb appropriate to the piece.' This, he thought, would ruin everything. I could fight the matter ofttimes successfully at rehearsal, and then would behold the check suit and hear all about Trinity Church when it came to the public performance.

Christmas Crackers

Humour is a difficult subject, as the worthy mayor discovered.
But then the Victorian sense of humour can be quite
unfathomable. I suppose that they thought it was funny – come
to think of it, the writers of Christmas cracker jokes still do.
Here is a selection of 'Christmas Crackers', guaranteed to have
readers of the Weston super Mare Gazette *in stitches in*
1894.

When may a thief be justly termed a gaol-bird? When he's been a robin.

Why should a baby never be taken into a painter's studio? Because of them easels.

Why is the remainder of a leg of mutton like Windsor? Because it is near eaten (Eton).

Why are temperance societies a bar to friendship? Because they prevent shaking hands.

What is the best way to make a thin child fat? Throw it out of the window and it will come down plump.

Why should a clergyman always wear well-fitting clothes? Because he should never be a man of loose habits.

How many young ladies will it take to reach from London to Brighton? Fifty-two, because a miss is as good as a mile.

What is the difference between a bantam cock and a dirty housemaid? One is a domestic fowl, and the other is a foul domestic.

Why are bonfires like grey-headed sinners? Because they scintillate (sin-till-late).

When has a man a right to scold his wife about his coffee? When he has sufficient grounds.

Why is a man seeking the company of conspirators like another going through a field where there are tall trees growing? Because he's going where there's high-trees-on (high treason).

Why is a watch which has been allowed to run down, through carelessness, like the Western Bank? Because, through bad management it has stopped, and consequently gives no more tick, and in order to set matters right, requires to be wound up.

What animal is that which in the morning goes upon four legs; in the afternoon upon two, and in the evening upon three? Man – in the morning of his life upon all-fours; in the afternoon on two; and in the evening with a stick.

Punch Night

W.G. WILLIS WATSON

Well, before it becomes any more contrived, perhaps we should draw a veil over Victorian humour – except to note in passing that the last one is as old as the Oedipus legend of ancient Greece. Perhaps the only time that 'Christmas Cracker' humour can seem even remotely funny is after a few glasses of punch. And that was a Somerset speciality on New Year's Eve. Here is Willis Watson again, warming to his subject.

This is the last day of the year. And many customs are associated with it. There is, of course, the bell-ringing — 'Ring out the old, Ring in the new'; there are the thousands of good wishes one proffers to the others, there are the merry parties — the seeing of the old year out and the new year in, and the clinking of glasses as the clock in the old church tower tells the midnight hour. Our forefathers knew how to enjoy themselves, and on no night in the year was greater merriment, greater conviviality, and greater good-will expressed than on New Year's Eve. It was on this night that the village inns were scenes of jollity and fun. Old Boniface was then seen at his best — his hospitality was unbounded.

Publicans are the *bêtes noires* of some folk, and the public house is looked upon as a sink of iniquity. But at this season of the year one may reflect that the infant Saviour would probably have been born in an inn if the crowded condition of the house had not forced the Holy Mother to seek shelter in an adjoining stable. And one wonders exceedingly why some professing Christians have such strong feelings against a house which represents the birth-place of Christ. The man who fell among thieves was taken to an inn, and his wounds dressed. Probably that is the reason why today, in country places, especially if one wishes to receive solace, comfort, and hospitality, one usually selects the village hostelry, and is not often disappointed at the reception accorded. But it is at Christmas-tide especially that the inn appeals to one's fancies. A picture which must ever attract the literary character is that of the Holly Tree Inn, drawn by Dickens. Here the guests were expected to join in the general 'convivials', rather than spend the idle hours alone with books.

It was in such a house as this that at Christmas-tide the bowl of punch used to circulate, and it was a liquor described by Dickens as, 'uncommonly good Punch!' Yes, the words bring back happy memories of my native town in Somerset. Then it was genial landlords and landladies were wont to

invite their customers on New Year's Eve to gather around the steaming bowl to partake of their hospitality, and, incidentally, to wish the worthy hosts the compliments of the season. The brewing of the punch was quite a ceremonial art. It was not concocted in a twentieth-century hurry, but deliberately each ingredient was carefully measured and mixed, and the brewing jealously guarded from outsiders. Its component parts were kept a family secret, and handed down by father to son, or, by purchase, from landlord to landlord of the inn which had earned a reputation for its punch.

There were many such houses in Somerset; but none stood higher in the county – or perhaps in the whole of England – than the George at Crewkerne, in the days of old Mrs Marsh, whose name and fame, fifty years ago, as a brewer of punch, pervaded the land. It is perpetuated in the pages of *Punch* that there were only two places at which real, genuine punch could be obtained – the one was at the George at Crewkerne; the other at *Punch* Office, Fleet Street. There are still inns situate in Somerset where the old-time custom of free punch is observed on New Year's Eve. 'Success to old England', was always drunk in a steaming glass of punch, and if ever there were a beverage associated with Britain this is one.

The custom of drinking punch on New Year's Eve only dates back to the latter part of the seventeenth century. But it soon established itself, and was proclaimed the 'King of Drinks', among its devotees being Fox and Sheridan and 'all the statesmen of the Whig party'. Not only was it a beverage with the idle rich, but the humble poor acquired the palate, and a punch bowl was found in the houses of many far beneath the rank and social status of the noble. The bowl often figured in the lists of wedding presents, and formed the gift bestowed upon men who had earned the respect and goodwill of their fellows. Punch accommodates itself to the means of all classes, rich and poor. As Leigh Hunt has said,

'You may have it of the costliest wine or the humblest malt liquor'. In many a hostelry in Somerset one sees the old punch bowl occupying a place of honour in the bar. It remains to be gazed upon all the year round, or until some special event is celebrated or New Year's Eve is honoured. Then it is taken down, carefully dusted, carried behind the scenes into an inner room or the kitchen – at all events away from the eyes of the public – and there the mystic rites are performed, something after the following formula:

> Whene'er a bowl of punch we make,
> Four striking opposites we take –
> The strong, the weak, the sour, the sweet,
> Together mixed, most kindly meet;
> And when they happily unite,
> The bowl is pregnant with delight.

Even now the secret is not revealed, for the old published recipes vary in an extraordinary degree, and what ingredient it is which made a certain punch here and there along the countryside in Somerset more famous than the other was ever jealously guarded. There is little doubt that the old bowl of punch on New Year's Eve is a continuation of the custom handed down from our Anglo-Saxon forefathers, who passed the wassail bowl on the vigil of the New Year to those assembled around the glowing hearth to drown every former animosity. Tonight in many an inn in dear old Somerset the punch bowl will be filled and pledges of friendship will be renewed, and a custom which has existed in this country for certainly over fourteen hundred years will be perpetuated.

In with the New

*Time for New Year celebrations now, and first a song. Cecil
Sharp, who led the folk-song collecting movement at the
beginning of this century, did much of his pioneer work in
Somerset, and rescued from oblivion a number of carols and
Christmas songs. This one he heard in Huish Episcopi, near
Langport, but very similar words were collected also at Othery
and Nether Stowey.*

I wish you a merry Christmas and a happy new year,
Your pockets full of money and your barrels full of beer;
So and I wish you all a happy new year, new year, new year,
So and I wish you all a happy new year.
The old year it is past and the new year it is come,
And all the jolly soldiers are beating on the drum;
So and I wish, etc., etc.

Here's a health to you in water, I wish it was in wine;
And all the money you have got, I'm sure it's none of mine;
So and I wish, etc., etc.

Here's a health unto our Master and Mistress likewise,
And all the pretty family around the fireside;
So and I wish you all a happy new year, new year, new year
So and I wish you all a happy new year.

*And now here is a very special New Year party, in fact a New
Century party. The details were written by a Frome journalist into
his diary of remarkable events.*

January 1st, 1801, the first day of the XIXth Century. We must begin the new century with Orchardleigh Masquerade; as that both finish'd the old, and began the new year.

Wednesday an elegant suite of apartments were thrown open at Orchardleigh House for the reception of masks, who, to the number of 200, assembled at an early hour. In order to heighten the hilarity of the entertainment, all dominos were excluded; the characters were numerous, and these, by their frequent change or [*sic*] dress, added apparently to the catalogue of merry mortals. Among the most prominent were – a Jeffery Wild-Goose, in search of his daughter; an owl; a lame fidler; Punch; a most beautiful figure in the dress of a Christ-hospital boy; a Fury, clothed in the terrors of infernal paraphernalia, pursuing an Orestes; two chattering barbers; a dancing bear; a pretty milk-maid; an elegant representative of a Fille de Patmos; and a French taylor, *bien habillé*, galloping on a very magnificent goose. This last mask was exquisite, and by the drollery of its appearance, and the novelty of its accoutrements, preserved its fascination throughout the whole of the diversion. There were a few elegant figures of both sexes, very splendidly dressed; and although the parade and insipidity of finery is inconsistent with the true genius of a masquerade, yet even this is less offensive than noisy nonsense and impertinent clamour. The supper was served in the richest profusion; but from a laudable attention to the severity of 'existing circumstances', the use of bread was entirely prohibited.

Three Glastonbury Thorn Stories

With the passing of the year it seems that Christmas is over. But not quite. In fact, by old Somerset reckoning – it hadn't even quite begun!

The leap year is a device to correct the discrepancy between the calendar and solar years. But for the sake of precision the leap year must be omitted once a century. Until the sixteenth century this was not properly understood, and by then there was some ten days' divergence. In Great Britain this was tolerated until 1752, in which year eleven days (3rd to 13th September) were entirely omitted from the calendar, so that the 2nd September was followed immediately by the 14th. This synchronized the calendar and solar years, but was resisted by many people, who thought that the government was trying to shorten their lives by eleven days. Fairs and feast days tended to honour the 'old style' dates, as they were known, by taking place eleven (or sometimes twelve) days later than the 'new style' would suggest they should. Consequently either 5th or 6th January, eleven or twelve days after 25th December, was regarded as the *real* Christmas Day, and was known as 'Old Christmas Day'. The resulting confusion gives us our cue to introduce perhaps the best loved of Somerset's Christmas folklore. This note appeared in the *Western Flying Post* in January 1753, the first Christmas after the alteration of the calendar.

By a letter from Glastonbury we hear that a vast concourse of people attended the thorn on Christmas Eve, new stile;

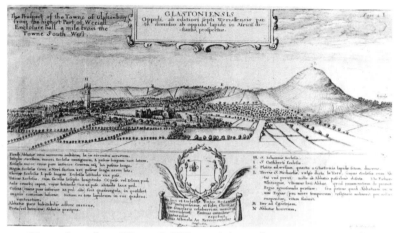

Glastonbury from Wearyall Hill, an eighteenth-century prospect by
Wenceslaus Hollar

but to their great disappointment, there was no appearance
of its blowing, which made them watch it narrowly the
fifth of January, the Christmas day, old stile, when it blowed
as usual and in one day's time was as white as a sheet, to the
great mortification of many families in that neighbourhood,
who had tapp'd their ale eleven days too soon.

The legend, in outline, tells us that Joseph of Arimathea
travelled as a missionary to Britain, and when faced by a
hostile crowd on Weary-all Hill next to Glastonbury he struck
his hawthorn staff into the ground. Miraculously it took root
and blossomed, and as a token of the truth of the Christian
message the Glastonbury thorn has continued to flower every
Christmas Day. Staffs becoming trees are found elsewhere in
Christian tradition, for example nearby in Wiltshire, where the
village of Bishopstrow ('the bishop's tree') is supposed to derive

St Joseph of Arimathea, a
woodcut by Mollie Power of a
window in Langport Church

its name from a legend that St Aldhelm's ashen staff turned
into an ash tree while he preached there. Presumably these
stories, as well as the survival in churchyards of yew trees
older than the earliest church on the site, suggest that in
such places Christianity supplanted a pagan observance
which included the veneration of trees. But the Christmas
flowering seems to have originated at Glastonbury. The
tradition existed by 1520, when a poem recounting the life
of Joseph of Arimathea was published. Here is the relevant
part.

Great meruaylles men may se at Glastenbury,
One of a walnot tree that there dooth stande,
In the holy grounde called the semetory,
Harde by the place where kynge Arthur was founde.
South fro Iosephs chapell it is walled in rounde,
It bereth no leaues tyll the day of saynt Barnabe
   [11th June];
And than that tree, that standeth in the grounde,
Spredeth his leaues as fayre as any other tree.

Thre hawthornes also, that groweth in werall [Weary-all],
Do burge and bere grene leaues at Christmas
As fresshe as other in May, when the nightyngale
Wrestes out her notes musycall as pure as glas;
Of all wodes and forestes she is the chefe chauntres.
In wynter to synge yf it were her nature,
In werall she myght haue a playne place,
On those hawthornes to shewe her notes clere.

Lo, lordes, what Ihesu dooth in Ianuary,
Whan the great colde cometh to grounde;
He maketh the hauthorne to sprynge full fresshely.
Where as it pleaseth hym, his grace is founde;
He may loose all thing that is bounde.
Thankes be gyuen to hym that in heuen sytteth,
That floryssheth his werkes so on the grounde,
And in Glastenbury, Quia mirabilia fecit
   ['because he performs wonders'].

It is notable that at this date the three miraculous hawthorns have not yet become linked to the Joseph of Arimathea legend; indeed Geoffrey Grigson has suggested that: 'The original story was no doubt that the Glastonbury Thorn or Thorns blossomed on Christmas day because hawthorn was the material of the

The Holy Thorn in Bloom, photographed at Christmas 1912, a few
months before Edward Thomas visited Glastonbury

crown of thorns.' The link with Joseph had been made by 1677,
and the present version of the legend dates from the eighteenth
century. Like the thorn itself, the legend has proved very
resilient to attack, and any hint of scepticism about either
would be quite out of place in the present context. Let us
instead ask the poet Edward Thomas, who visited Glastonbury
at Easter 1913, to use the legend to transport us from the
miracle of Christmas to the hope of Spring.

At first I thought I should not see more of the abbey than
can be seen from the road – the circular abbot's kitchen
with pointed cap, and the broken ranges of majestic tall
arches that guide the eye to the shops and dwellings of
Glastonbury. While I was buying a postcard the woman

of the shop reminded me of Joseph of Arimathea's thorn, and how it blossomed at Christmas. 'Did you ever see it blossoming at Christmas?' I asked. 'Once,' she said, and she told me how the first winter she spent at Glastonbury was a very mild one, and she went out with her brothers for a walk on Christmas day in the afternoon. She remembered that they wore no coats. And they saw blossom on the holy thorn. After all, I did go through the turnstile to see the abbey. The high pointed arches were magnificent, the turf under them perfect. The elms stood among the ruins like noble savages among Greeks. The orchards hard by made me wish that they were blossoming. But excavations had been going on; clay was piled up and cracking in the sun, and there were tin sheds and scaffolding. I am not an archaeologist, and I left it. As I was approaching the turnstile an old hawthorn within a few yards of it, against a south wall,

The Holy Thorn in April, 1912

drew my attention. For it was covered with young green leaves and with bright crimson berries almost as numerous. Going up to look more closely, I saw what was more wonderful – Blossom. Not one flower, nor one spray only, but several sprays. I had not up till now seen even blackthorn flowers, though towards the end of February I had heard of hawthorn flowering near Bradford. As this had not been picked, I conceitedly drew the conclusion that it had not been observed. Perhaps its conspicuousness had saved it. It was Lady Day. I had found the Spring in that bush of green, white, and crimson. So warm and bright was the sun, and so blue the sky, and so white the clouds, that not for a moment did the possibility of Winter returning cross my mind.

The Final Word

WALTER RAYMOND

But, wait a minute! This is a book about Christmas, not a book about Spring. Walter Raymond, who doubtless could have filled a whole book with his own memories of Somerset Christmases, can have the honour of the last word.

It wanted but one day to Christmas Day, and for some time signs of the approach of that festive season had multiplied in

Sutton. Ever since November, twice a week instead of once, had the ringers practised 'for Christmas'. Ever since the beginning of the month small parties of children had crept quietly into porches or on to doorsteps, hoping to earn a penny by singing carols. There came a shuffling of feet, a little half-suppressed cough, and their voices, both shrill and nasal, burst out:

> Good Keeng Wenceslas looked out
> On the Feast of Stephen,
> When the snow lay round about
> Dee-pan crip-san –

By this time the door would open. 'Go away, you noisy children you. Kirsmas idden here yet.' And with this the door would slam and all become silent again for a few minutes, until fainter by distance:

> Good Keeng Wen –

'Tormenten little images!' cried Mrs Josiah Heppell for the twentieth time. 'Did really ought to be stopped. To be sure the choir do come round o' Christmas Eve, an' that's well enough. For they don't come till midnight an' then we be all sound asleep. For folk don't bide up to have the singers in, same as they did the mummers an' all when I was a maid at home. In cou'se, there idden no mummers now, an' the carol singers 'ud soonest not come inside. Because why, if they do, they can't find the face to call round day after Christmas with the book.'

Yet signs of festivity were not altogether absent. Carts laden with red-berried holly passed down the village street on the way to Oldbury. Young John Brook brought the best part of a load for the decoration of Sutton Church; and Miss Letty Purchase stood out on the causeway and bargained in public for 'a misseltoe' that Selina Jane Edwards described as 'half as big

as a house'. Pearls were set between its golden-green leaves as thick as stars in the firmament. 'Massy 'pon us!' cried the old Betsy Mogridge. 'Why, if you can find a use for all they berries, missie, verily an' truly there won't be none o' ee left – an can't.' For the old notion was that a berry must be picked off for every kiss, and when the berries were gone there was an end to it.

Mrs Josiah Heppell was serving my last evening repast. It was later than usual, because I had loitered with Shepherd. The lamp was lighted. The blinds were drawn. I no longer sat in the window, but comfortably by the fire, and for the last week this excellent woman had not enjoyed the advantage of a view of the street. But as the blind are said to receive some compensation for their loss of sight in the alertness of the other senses, so, it appeared to me, this deprivation had but made the hearing of Mrs Josiah Heppell abnormally acute.

'But sure,' said she, 'we shall miss ee when you be gone, for, as Japheth Pike said to Heppell only last week, though maybe I didn' ought to mention, yet said all in kindness too, "I really do admire how he do go about an' poke his nose into everything." He really did, though no harm meant or taken, I do hope indeed— Harky then! There's the rumble o' wheels. Then that's Mrs Treloar, Baker Heath's wife's mother. A elderly lady an' lame o' the left foot, though well off, as 'tis said, an' very genteel for certain, come every year in a hired conveyance. Yes, there, the fly have a-stopped. She do come from down the country, always the day afore, out o' the hurry-push o' folk fo'ced to bide for business— Yes, an' I *do* hope you'll come to Sutton again one o' these days, an' the room, if not let, always ready, an' pleased we always should be, or any friend, if you should ever be able to recommend— There's the slam o' the workshop door. Then carpenter have a-made firm the leg o' the tressel for the handbell ringers— An' to be sure we did hope you would bide Christmas. Though Christmas is nothing now but the coming home o' friends, an', I do

Walter Raymond, in old age

suppose you do think you must go home so well as the rest—
Lauk! There's a cackle o' fowls then. That's young John Brook
choosing a couple off the roost. He do keep crossed wi' the
game. Send a couple every year to his sister to Oldbury. Ah!
kill 'em so as to catch the moment to send in unpicked by the
Oldbury fly, I'll warrant it. Though, if I might make so bold
– but maybe I ought not to tell – and yet more convenient to
know for certain sure, for what so ill-convenient as to be taken
on the hop? But the handbell ringers, they did think to— An'
that's Japheth. I do know his step. He do hit one heel harder
than t'other on the flagstone. He'll put his head in an' holler
to smith, an' they'll be here in ten minutes—'

'Who will be here, Mrs Heppell?'

'The handbell ringers. They do go about Sutton at
Christmas, an', of course, they must come in with the bells, if
you didn't mind. An' the book is for the church ringers—'

'Of course, they must come in, Mrs Heppell. Make haste,

my good woman. Run for your life. Scald out the washhand basin. Bring up the soup-ladle. Get glasses. Get spoons. Get lemons. Get sugar. Bustle, I tell you, and put on the biggest kettle to your name.'

'What for?' asked Mrs Josiah Heppell, in surprise.

'Because I am an artist, woman. Because I am a genius at it—'

'At what?'

'At the brewing of punch.'

'Then my old Aunt Juke's old blue bowl 'ud be better,' said she, 'an' I'll fetch un up from parlour table to once. Hark! There they be, then, by the scuffle. An' that's the tressels dapped down till Heppell do ope the door. I'd better to run—'

She ran.

The handbell ringers came quietly. They set up their board and tressels and arranged their bells in a subdued whisper. And gradually acquaintances who were not ringers slyly found their way into the room, which was large enough indeed to hold the whole parish. At last, it seemed that we were all there. For Uncle Dick went driving past and Heppell stopped him, and Dairyman, having an errand into the village, was pulled in by force. Somebody ran to borrow glasses at the Manor Farm and to ask Mr William Purchase to step across.

The Sutton handbell ringers rang carols on the bells very sweetly and proceeded to 'The Missletoe Bough' and other Christmas ballads. By that time the water boiled. The old room was filled with the fragrance of lemons and, well, of other things. Old Aunt Juke's old blue bowl was a jewel. Likely enough it had seen orgies in its time. Did the unexpected warmth from the biggest kettle revive old memories, I wonder? At least it brought goodwill to that little company, and an hour of old-fashioned jollity.

'Merry Christmas!'

'Merry Christmas!'

We held aloft our glasses, and it was merry Christmas everywhere.

Then we got to songs and at last to choruses. All the little trumpery differences of the past year were swept away and Heppell even smiled upon young John Brook.

And when the bowl was empty it was filled again, until at last it came to 'Good-night'..

'Good-night.'

'Though I am very much afraid,' said one, 'it must be — good-bye.'

And so, 'Good-bye'.

'Good-bye.'

Acknowledgements

The compilation of this book has taxed the patience and expertise of librarians and archivists in Somerset and elsewhere, and I offer them my warmest thanks. I am particularly grateful to the staff of Bath, Bristol and Weston super Mare Reference Libraries (Avon Library and Information Service); Somerset Local History Library and Yeovil Reference Library (Somerset County Council Library Service); Somerset Archaeological and Natural History Society; the Somerset Record Office, Taunton; and the Trowbridge Local Studies Library (Wiltshire County Council, Library & Museum Service). I most gratefully acknowledge the permission to publish copyright material, granted by the copyright owners specifically listed below, and apologize to any other copyright owners whose rights I have unwittingly infringed. I owe special debts of gratitude for help and advice to the following individuals: Robin Ansell, Sue Berry, David Bromwich, Liz Clark, Bob Dunning, Adam Green, Steve Hobbs, Katy Jordan, Ian Patey, Bob Patten and Bruce Watkin; and of course for her constant encouragement to my wife, Alison.

'Exmoor's Winter Pageant' is from *Wild Exmoor through the Year*, by E.W. Hendy, 1930, pp.290–3. 'An Admiral's Childhood' is from *Two Admirals*, by John Moresby, 1909, pp.36–9. 'The Wassailing Party' is from *Tales of the Blackdown Borderland*, by F.W. Mathews (Somerset Folk Series, 13), pp.118–29. 'Catching the Words' and 'A Peculiar Witchery' are from the 1912 edition of *Tryphena in Love* and *Young Sam and Sabina*, by Walter Raymond, pp.110–13 and 150–55. 'Here Comes I. . .' is a transcript of a broadside in the Somerset Record Office (SRO DD/SAS C/2273 3/4), reproduced by kind permission of the Somerset Archaeological and Natural History Society (hereafter SA&NHS); other plays will be found in *Somerset and the Drama*, by S.R. Littlewood (Somerset Folk Series, 7), pp.97–9; and *Somerset County Herald*, 16.12.1922. 'Mrs Comfort's Party' is from *Lewisham Newsletter*, Easter 1928, pp.14–15 (copy in Weston super Mare Local Studies Library). 'The Week before Christmas' is from *A Somerset Sketch Book*, by H. Hay Wilson, 1912, pp.128–37. 'Muscatels in Clusters' was compiled from issues of the *Weston super Mare Gazette* and *Weston Mercury and Somersetshire Herald*, 15.12.1894 and 22.12.1894. 'The First Christmas Card' is by John Chandler, derived principally from *Fifty*

Years of Public Work of Sir Henry Cole, 2 vols., 1884; *Dictionary of National Biography*; *The History of the Christmas Card*, by George Buday, 1954; *Notes and Queries*, 9th series, vol.12, 14.11.1903; various newspaper cuttings among the 'Local Notes and Queries' files in Somerset Local History Library. 'Christmas at the Post Office' is from the *Weston Mercury and Somersetshire Herald*, 29.12.1894. 'A Withered Rose' is from 'An Old-Fashioned Christmas' by Alice King, in *Home Chimes*, December, 1891, pp.363–9 (offprint in a bound volume entitled *Papers by Alice King* in SA&NHS Library). 'Songs Ancient and Curious' was compiled from various sources, as follows: the Bridgwater carol, reproduced by kind permission of Bridgwater Charter Trustees, is in the Somerset Record Office (SRO D/B/bw 123), and has been published in *Bridgwater Borough Archives*, vol.5, 1971, edited by R.W. Dunning and T.D. Tremlett (Somerset Record Society, vol.70), pp.6–7; 'I bought a cock. . .' was printed in *Somerset County Herald*, 22.12.1922; the Frome carol is in the Somerset Record Office (SRO DD/SAS C/2401/32) and is reproduced by kind permission of SA&NHS; Thomas Shoel is described in *Somerset Essays*, by Llewelyn Powys, 1937, pp.134–5, and the poem is from *Poems by Thomas Shoel*, 1821, pp.109–11; 'The earth has donned. . .' by W.W. Butler, appears in a handwritten school magazine, *The Eagle*, vol.1, issue of 9.12.1901, pp.10–11, in Weston super Mare Local Studies Library; 'The Holly Boy and the Ivy Girl' is printed in *Somerset Folklore*, by R.L. Tongue, 1965 (Folklore Society, vol.114), pp.209–10, and is reproduced with kind permission of the Folklore Society and the executors of Ruth Tongue. 'Not like the Old Days' is from *Calendar of customs, superstitions, weather-lore. . . connected with the county of Somerset*, by W.G. Willis Watson, 1920, pp.459–62. 'North Curry Reeve's Feast' is abridged from *North Curry: Ancient Manor and Hundred*, by H.P. Olivey, 1901, pp.11–20. 'A Wet Christmas' is from *To the Radical Reformers, Male and Female, of England, Scotland, and Ireland*, by Henry Hunt, no.13 (24.12.1821). 'The Turkeys and the Butcher' is from Somerset Record Office (SRO Q/SR 156/28 and Q/SO 7, f.373), and is Crown Copyright material reproduced by permission of the Controller of Her Majesty's Stationery Office. 'Lightning Attack' is from *Somerset and Dorset Notes and Queries*, vol.3, pp.275–6, quoting the *Postmaster* (Exeter), 8.1.1726. 'A Passing Animal' is from *Somerset and Dorset Notes and Queries*, vol.4, pp.45–7, quoting *Western Gazette*, 5.1.1894. 'The Snow Dumpling' is from *Some Ballad-Legends of Somerset*, by D.M. Cary, 1924 (Somerset Folk Series, 14), pp.118–19 (the quotation from a Glastonbury history is in Somerset Record Office, SRO DD/SAS SE82, opposite appendix p.i, and is quoted by kind permission of

SA&NHS). 'The Old Man's Christmas Story' is from *Ghosts and Legends of South Somerset*, by G.F. Munford, 1922 (Somerset Folk Series, 3), pp.21–30. 'A Black Day' is taken, by kind permission of Gerald Duckworth & Co. Ltd, from *A City of Bells*, by Elizabeth Goudge, 1936. 'The Missletoe Bough' is taken by kind permission of the County Archivist, Adam Green, from the version transcribed in Somerset Record Office SRO D/P/baw 23/2 (see also D.M. Cary, *op.cit.* pp.93–4). 'Burnham-on-Santa' is from *Burnham-on-Sea Gazette*, 15.12.1945. 'The Waning of Bethlehem's Star' is by John Chandler, drawing information from *Rutland Boughton and the Glastonbury Festivals*, by Michael Hurd, 1993; sleeve notes by Michael Hurd to Rutland Boughton's *Bethlehem* (Hyperion CDA66690); Littlewood, S.R. *op.cit.*, pp.102–3; and *Central Somerset Gazette*, 22.7.1927, p.5. 'The Dark Visitor' is extracted from W.G. Willis Watson, *op.cit.* 'Oh, No, It Isn't!' is compiled from *Bath Chronicle*, 26.12.1850; 2.1.1851; and *In the days of Victoria*, by Thomas F. Plowman, 1918, pp.207–9. 'Christmas Crackers' is from *Weston super Mare Gazette*, 22.12.1894. 'Punch Night' is from W.G. Willis Watson, *op.cit.*, pp.475–8. 'In with the New' is from *Folk Songs from Somerset*, by Cecil Sharp, 5th series, 1909, pp.70–71, 91; and Somerset Record Office (SRO DD/SAS C/2710) which is reproduced by kind permission of SA&NHS. 'Three Glastonbury Thorn Stories' is by John Chandler, quoting material from W.G. Willis Watson, *op.cit.*, p.8; *Joseph of Arimathie. . .*, edited by W.W. Skeat (Early English Text Society), 1871, p.49; and *In Pursuit of Spring*, by Edward Thomas, 1914, pp. 252–3; see also *Glastonbury Abbey. . .*, by James P. Carley, 1988, pp.181–4; and *The Englishman's Flora*, by Geoffrey Grigson, 1955, p.170. 'The Final Word' is from *English Country Life*, by Walter Raymond, 1910, pp.436–43.

Picture Credits

Except where otherwise credited illustrations are from the collections held at Somerset Local History Library, and are reproduced by kind permission of Somerset Archaeological and Natural History Society (SA&NHS) or Somerset County Council Library Service (SCC). My grateful thanks are extended not only to these two organizations, but also to David Bromwich and Derek Parker who processed the photographs.

Pages 2; 4; 6; 14; 19; 32 (from SRO DD/SAS S/141); 40; 43; 62; 74; 90; 94; 99; 125 and 127 (from SRO DD/SAS S/141); 137; 140; 141; 145 – SA&NHS. Pages 10; 47; 65 – SCC. Page 22 – from *Somerset Yearbook*, 1934, opp. p.96. Page 116 – from *Somerset Yearbook*, 1936, p.59. Pages 117 and 119 – from *Somerset Yearbook*, 1935, pp.99, 101. Page 138 – from *Somerset Yearbook*, 1930, p.87. Page 25 – from *Somerset Countryman*, Jan. 1938, p.24. Pages 51 and 56 – from *Fifty Years of Public Work of Sir Henry Cole*, 1884. Page 69 – Bridgwater Charter Trustees (SRO D/B/bw 123). Page 83 – N.R. Chipchase. Page 86 – compiler. Page 88 – from *Investigations at Ilchester Gaol*, 1821. Page 104 – from E.W. Hendy, *Wild Exmoor through the Year*, 1930.